PURE GOLD

BOBBY BOWDEN

As told to

STEVE ELLIS AND BILL VILONA

SP
SPORTS
PUBLISHING
L.L.C.

SportsPublishingLLC.com

ISBN-10: 1-59670-120-x
ISBN-13: 978-1-59670-120-5

Publishers: Peter L. Bannon and Joseph J. Bannon Sr.
Senior managing editor: Susan M. Moyer
Acquisitions editor: Mike Pearson
Developmental editor: Mark Newton
Art director: K. Jeffrey Higgerson
Dust jacket design: Joseph Brumleve
Interior layout: Dustin J. Hubbart
Photo editor: Erin Linden-Levy

Sports Publishing L.L.C.
804 North Neil Street
Champaign, IL 61820
Phone: 1-877-424-2665
Fax: 217-363-2073
SportsPublishingLLC.com

Printed in the United States of America

Library of Congress Cataloging-in-Publication Data

Ellis, Steve.
  Bobby Bowden : an inside look / as told to Steve Ellis and William D. Vilona.
    p. cm.
  ISBN-13: 978-1-59670-120-5 (hard cover : alk. paper)
  ISBN-10: 1-59670-120-X (hard cover : alk. paper)
  1. Bowden, Bobby. 2. Football coaches--United States. 3. Florida State University--Football. 4. Florida State Seminoles (Football team) I. Vilona, William D. II. Title.
GV939.B66E55 2006
796.332092--dc22
[B]

                        2006023415

CONTENTS

FOREWORD

The Florida State football team would stay in my hometown, Thomasville, Georgia, on the nights before their home games. I would always see them coming in on those nights, but I never thought I would be on that bus one day, playing for Coach Bobby Bowden. I will always be grateful that he took a chance on me.

But more importantly, Coach Bowden is a great example of a man of integrity and a man of God. I believe that will be his legacy.

Coach Bowden and his assistants provided a good atmosphere for a young man to grow. The coaches I was around would get on us, but it wasn't like every other word was a curse word. If you are around something like that a lot, you tend to pick up those same bad habits. The people who Coach Bowden surrounded himself with and the attitude that they created played a big part in our success.

On Friday nights before games, we would have devotion. Devotion was short, but it was a good way to kick off the preparation for our game. Coach Bowden allowed a chaplain around us a lot, and I believe that was important for us. I know it was important for me to be in that kind of situation and to have that kind of leader in Coach Bowden.

My first memory of Coach Bowden was when he came into our house during recruiting. He was very laid back, and once we got to talking to him, he started going off on all these one-liners and stories. I lived only 30 miles from Tallahassee and had watched Florida State for so long—just to have him in our living room was an honor.

I learned then that Coach Bowden was a man who kept his word. During my recruiting, he shared with me that if I held up my end of the bargain as far as my responsibilities to football and the classroom, he would allow me to play basketball if I had the opportunity and chose to do it. A lot of coaches said they would allow me to also play basketball but didn't have the history of allowing players to play two sports. Coach Bowden said, "I want you to concentrate on football, but I will let you play both."

It certainly meant a lot to me that he kept his word. A lot of coaches would not have kept it once they had me in school. I do believe that.

Another thing he shared with me during my recruiting was that there were two quarterbacks in front of me. He wanted to make certain I understood that. I was given an opportunity to play quarterback my freshman year and to compete for the job, but the other quarterbacks were ahead of me in experience. Because of what Coach Bowden told me, I understood the situation coming in. I was fine with that. At that time, the playing time was mostly going to those with seniority. But he was as fair as he possibly could be, and he tried to get those who deserved an opportunity that chance to play.

Sometimes that opportunity did not come until later on, and Coach Bowden told me I would have to be patient. He told me I would be given a chance, and that happened to a degree because Coach Bowden was willing to change. He went to an offense that was different from the one he was accustomed to running. He had an idea of the new system, but he didn't have a firm grasp of it. For me, that was a big thing—that he would be willing to change his offense after having been so successful with another for so many years.

He gave his assistants so much responsibility. Even when he did have a hand in calling the plays on offense, he allowed the position coaches to do so much. He was patient with his staff, and we were able to work with the new offense and come up with the system that would cause confusion for the defense.

We were able to have a lot of success. It was good to win the first national championship at Florida State because Coach Bowden had been so close in previous years. It was great to be a part of something he really deserved. And it was good to be able to win the first Heisman Trophy for Florida State. Of course, Coach Bowden was a big part of my being the recipient of the Heisman Trophy, as were my teammates and the other coaches.

Our success—the winning—came from guys buying into the system and doing what Coach Bowden and his coaches asked us to do.

It came from us trusting one another. Coach Bowden always stressed the team, and the guys put in their work. One of the good things about Coach Bowden is that he didn't put a lot of pressure on us about winning and didn't talk a lot about it. He stressed more about taking care of things you can take care of: the fundamentals and teamwork.

It is an honor to enter the College Football Hall of Fame with Coach Bowden. We will always be Hall of Fame classmates, and I am grateful that I had an opportunity to play for him. It was a great experience.

—Charlie Ward, 1993 Heisman Trophy winner; 11-year NBA player

ACKNOWLEDGMENTS

Thanks to all who gave their time to interview with us and who gave us so much more material than we could have ever included in one volume. Your contributions were great and made the editing process a labor of love.

Thanks also to Bob Ferrante for his tireless work in helping this book become a reality.

T. K. WETHERELL

THE PRESIDENT

Some roles may have reversed for T. K. Wetherell, but the admiration he has for Bobby Bowden has not changed in the more than 30 years they have known each other. Wetherell answered to Bowden when he arrived on the Florida State campus in the 1960s on a football scholarship. Bowden was then an assistant coach in charge of receivers on Bill Peterson's staff, which was full of future college and NFL head coaches.

Wetherell was a wide receiver who became part of the longest kickoff return in school history when he took a lateral and dashed 100 yards for a score against Kentucky in 1964.

Bowden took on the challenge of rebuilding FSU's football program in 1976, and Wetherell set out to do some building of his own. He became president of Tallahassee Community College in 1995, and in seven years he saw the school's enrollment and campus double in size. The former Florida House of Representative and House Speaker played an important role in the building of the University Center, which surrounds Bobby Bowden Field at Doak Campbell Stadium.

Wetherell became president of Florida State University and Bowden's boss in January 2003.

It was August of 1963 during two-a-days. I was a freshman wide receiver at Florida State. After practice that first day, the wide receivers were practicing crackback blocks. The key to a crackback block is keeping the defensive end from knowing you're coming. Once I'd practiced them for 20 minutes, defensive ends Jim Causey and George D'Alessandro and the others pretty well figured out what I was doing. And most of these guys were upperclassmen, so they really knew that from the start. By the time the deal was over, I think I had a broken nose and was looking out of the side of my helmet.

For about 20 minutes, we got the pure hell kicked out of us by this nice guy named Bobby Bowden. He was coaching the wide receivers, and that was the first time I ever met him.

For those of us coming out of high school to big-time college football—FSU really wasn't big-time then, but we thought it was—Bobby Bowden was like our head coach in high school. Everybody in college was like a head coach. And in Coach Bowden's case, he had been a head coach at Samford before he joined Florida State as an assistant coach. He knew what he was talking about. He was very precise and knew exactly what he wanted. He didn't write things in a notepad like he does now. He told you, and you listened and did it, or you didn't play. He saw everything.

He started us with basics. As a receiver, you had to get in the right stance to start with—inside foot back—and your head had to be up. If you got down like you were going to sprint out with your head down, he would run a cornerback up there who would just knock the crap out of you.

When we ran routes, he had a white line out there on the field, and we ran down that white line when we made a break so we didn't drift. I actually made the varsity based on my blocking ability more than my catching ability. I couldn't catch a cold. We had to block. We had to play with intensity. We had to do it all.

Coach Bowden was animated—very intense. He was involved in scrimmages, and back then they were pretty spirited affairs. We'd get in fights. Everybody was chewing tobacco and spitting on each other. Coaches got in the middle to pull people off the pile. It was a different world back then.

Coach Bowden would chew us up one side and then down the other if we didn't perform up to his expectations. During the games, he was always on the sideline. I remember playing against Houston in

1965, and we had a play where the receiver tripped and fell down, and the defensive back would run away. And then all of a sudden, we would throw the ball over there. I did that. Quarterback Ed Pritchett rolled out, and I got up and was 25 yards behind everybody. It was something else. Pritchett threw this beautiful pass, and it just floated up there, and I said to myself, "I got this puppy." I throttled it back a little bit, and that ball started coming down more like a punt, and I realized I had misjudged the throw. I turned the afterburners back on but missed it off the tip of my fingers.

I looked at Bowden on the sideline, and he started on me the moment I began jogging over there. I sat out three series before he put me back in.

ARE YOU JUST STUPID?

My first year on the varsity was my sophomore year, and our first game was against Texas Christian. We put in this play called 60 Divide. We started running that play during summer school. On the 60 route, I was supposed to run a curl route or zero route. But this was a divide, which meant we were going to do something different. I would run an out. Our tight end would run a curl; and our running back, Larry Green, would hit the middle of that seam. We practiced that play all summer long, all through two-a-days. And we practiced it against what Texas Christian was going to show on opening day. It was perfect in practice. Green would be all alone every time, and we would throw to him.

We got into the Texas Christian game and fell behind 7–3 in the fourth quarter. The 60 Divide was set up perfectly—left hash, 35-yard line. We called 60 Divide, and I went in there and ran the wrong zero route and ran flat into Larry Green. The ball bounced off of Larry's helmet, and Texas Christian intercepted the ball and almost scored.

I ran off the field, and there was Coach Bowden staring at me and saying, "Are you just stupid or something?"

We lost that game 7–3.

I never saw him get really angry. Even with the 60 Divide failure, it was more of him just standing there and wondering, "How in the heck can we work on this play for six months and mess it up?" His patience came in part because he had been a player only five years earlier. It hadn't been that long since he had been out there. Coach Bowden could remember what it was like to be in our shoes.

I don't remember him being that much of a screamer, but he was intense. Back then, if we ran an out route, we tried to get an outside position on the opposing player. Coach Bowden was not as fast as he thought he was, but sometimes he'd get out there and try to show us. We would all get a big chuckle out of that because he was 5-foot-5, and he was trying to show us how he did it at Samford. Yeah, right.

But afterward, when practice was over, he would always come through the locker room and talk to us. And except for him, nobody would come in the freshman locker room. He'd ask things like "How are you doing? How's your arm?" and say, "I know you got hurt," "You did good," or "You need to work on this."

TO THE BOWDENS' FOR HAMBURGERS

On Sundays, all the receivers would go over to his house. In the morning, most of us went to church, and most everybody went to First Baptist Church downtown. It was a good place to get dates. Bobby went to get saved. We went to get dates. It was a big social event, and then afterward, if you wanted to get free food, you'd go by Bobby's. Other coaches such as Bob Harbison and Bill Proctor did the same thing for their players. Coach Bowden and Ann lived off of Lakeshore Drive and they would feed us hamburgers and hot dogs each Sunday.

Most of us hunted back then, so we would leave our shotguns over there. We would go dove hunting or duck hunting. We never ran out of shells. There were always cases of shells for us. I remember bringing guns out there but no shells. That was just the way it was back then.

All those coaches on Bill Peterson's staff were great coaches. It was great to have Bowden, Don James, who coached all those years at Washington, and Joe Gibbs, Dan Henning, and Bill Parcells, who of

President T. K. Wetherell has witnessed many of his former coach's milestones, including the naming of Bobby Bowden Field on November 20, 2004. Ann Bowden was at Wetherell's side during the ceremony.
Courtesy of FSU Sports Information

course, all went to the NFL. The staff also included John Coatta and Bill Crutchfield, and you could just go down the list. With Bowden and that group in the '60s, we were preparing a game plan that was advanced for its time.

We walked on the field, and it was like a bunch of Einsteins from a football standpoint. A lot of people on defense were still running the Oklahoma 5-4 with a monster. If you put a pro offense up against that, you can throw backside routes all day long, particularly when you have Fred Biletnikoff as your receiver and Steve Tensi throwing. It was like taking candy away from a baby.

People just weren't running that stuff, so the things they were showing us were cutting-edge tactics for colleges. It was way ahead of the time. And they prepared us to play like pro teams. We knew tendencies. It was like we had an unfair advantage; we knew what the opponent was going to do.

LIKE A ROCK STAR

Coach "Bear" Bryant was the deal back then. I don't think anybody then realized the level Coach Bowden could reach.

He's like a rock star. When you go somewhere with the guy, it's almost like you have to have someone escorting him through the crowd, or he'll be there forever. We went down to the Seminole Tribe in February for an awards ceremony, and two hours later he was still standing around signing autographs. That's just the way it is with Coach Bowden.

I don't think anybody envisioned him getting to this level—being such a celebrity.

I think one thing that Bobby has done there, and it's probably what he's been criticized for the most in his later years, is that he doesn't give up on someone. Never give up—whether it's on a play, a game, or a person—that was a part of Bowden that was the mind-set of all those coaches under Bill Peterson. As coach and a player, you were loyal to the team. You did the best you could do. What was not acceptable was not giving 100 percent and not being loyal. When you look at Bobby, he'll give you one or two chances. At some point, he'll give up on you. It all works off the assumption that Coach Bowden wants to be fair with you but expects you to be fair with him. You walk in and say, "Yeah, I did it. I don't know why I did it. I'm stupid."

And he'll say, "Well, OK. Let's not do it again."

And I think there are limits he'll accept, as there are with anybody. I think he understands he's taking a bunch of 18-, 19-, and 20-year-old student-athletes who are in the public light and are put under a microscope. Coach Bowden will stick with you as long as you say, "This is my plan to change." If it's alcohol abuse, he'll go to Alcoholics Anonymous with that person if that's what it takes, as long as you're willing to make the effort. If you quit, he'll quit.

I didn't drink that much in college. I was always the designated driver. The problem is I got credit for being at most of the stuff mainly because I was the only one who could drive, and I'd have someone sitting in the back of the pickup shooting out stoplights downtown. We did some stuff that is just handled differently today. The press didn't really mess with our personal lives. That was kind of off-limits back then. Even when somebody got into trouble, they went to a coach, and the coach would solve that problem. Usually, the coach would run guys who got in trouble up those stairs until they puked, and they wouldn't do whatever it was again. Coach Bowden would be at the bottom of the steps at five o'clock in the morning. If you even jogged, he would start counting over again.

Now every time I mess up or do something he thinks is wrong, he'll just send me a message or say to me, "60 Divide." And when he does something that I think he's messed up—I send the same message. When he ran a fourth-and-1 in the Orange Bowl against Penn State, I asked him if *that* was a 60 Divide or what?

FROM PLAYER TO BOSS

It's a strange phenomenon to be working with the coach from my playing days, particularly because of who he is. Those kinds of relationships are rare. It's strange for me sometimes. He listens a lot more than I thought he would. But once he makes up his mind, I'm not going to change it. He leaves no doubts about where he is on something; he'll tell you.

He's not going to back off that, but I think he will temper it a little bit. I think Bowden has become more sensitive about what he says.

It's easier for me to talk to him about issues than it is with some people. He looks at me as somebody who played for him and also somebody who has played the game. What Bobby doesn't care much about is a bunch of sportswriters telling him what he ought to be doing. If an athlete walks in his office—particularly one who played for him—and says, "Why don't you do this?" or "Have you thought about this?"—he'll pay more attention to that.

Since I've been here, in all honesty, we haven't disagreed on anything. If he had his druthers, we would maybe have done some things a little differently. But if he made his pitch and got his fair shot, he was OK. He's been around universities a long time, and he knows presidents or the board of trustees have the last say. He understands pressure from boosters and money issues.

The one thing you don't ever have to worry about is Bobby asking for a pay raise. He'll fight for his coaches. But money for him is not in his vocabulary. If we paid a dollar, he would do the job. If other head coaches are making two dollars, then he wants two. Money is just a way to keep score, and as long as you're keeping it the same as everybody else, then he's fine.

The public keeps wanting to know what Coach Bowden is really like. How is he different? What you see on TV is what you see on the field or off it. There's no ego. Everybody will tell you one way or another that he's the same on national TV as he is sitting down and eating a hamburger.

Coach Bowden is totally absorbed with the game. We've talked how the game has changed in my mind. I used to go get a hot dog, hamburger, and Coca-Cola and look at plays being run. Now I figure out which donors are here and what the gate is like, and look around to make sure there are no fights in the end zone. I hardly see the game anymore. Coach Bowden was interested in how I could go to a football game and not focus on football. I told him a football game is a way to raise money and not a source of entertainment for me.

He said, "I don't think I could do that." And he reacted that way because he is so totally absorbed in the game. When I see him standing on the sideline, it's amazing how much he picks up—particularly being on the sideline, where you really can't see the game. But he's totally involved. He hears and sees a lot more than you'd think.

THE MOST VULNERABLE I'VE SEEN HIM

I think the way Coach Bowden is doing it today is a little bit different than how he was doing it 10 years ago or 30 years ago. But if he's going to do it, he's going to do it first class. When I first got the job here as president in 2003, my wife, Ginger, was with me on the team plane. We got back in at 4:00 a.m., and Bowden was shaving and washing and getting ready to do a TV show, break down film, and then go meet recruits.

Ginger isn't the greatest sports fan. She goes to the games and understands it better than she used to, and she said, "That guy is nearly 75 years old, and I can barely keep my eyes open, and he's getting ready to go on TV. How does he do it?"

I think he regenerates in July and doesn't do anything. But from August 1 until the bowl game, he is 24-7. He hasn't slowed down.

The criticism of his son Jeff weighs on him. There's no doubt it weighs on the man. When I got here, he was a lot more open. Maybe it's the Jeff stuff. Maybe it's the two or three seasons that haven't been what he wanted. He's a lot more guarded today than he was three years ago. All things considered, with the high expectations, I can understand that.

The death of his grandson, Bowden, and former son-in-law, John Madden, in that automobile accident the week before the 2004 Miami game probably had more impact on him than anything I've seen. He would just walk off into the stadium, and I'd see him sitting on the bleachers during a practice by himself. He can deal with a lot. I don't know if he knew how to deal with that. It was tough on him to deal with. That's the most vulnerable I ever saw him.

We flew to the funeral in Panama City with them. I think the only way they got through it was with family, and that family is really, really tight. They spent a lot of time, when I was there, all talking football. The sons, Tommy, Jeff, and Terry, would talk about this game or that game. They were about to have a service, and Bobby and Jeff were sitting there and saying, "Tommy, you couldn't run a blitz on third-and-whatever," or "I can't believe you ran that play."

It's just how they dealt with it; it wasn't callous. The loss of family shook them more than anything, but that's the way they dealt with it—through football and their faith. They immersed themselves in football and used football to get through that time.

In his mind, Bobby had to coach the next game in Miami. We were prepared for that not to happen—for Coach Bowden not to coach. And we assumed Mickey Andrews would step in and take over. The offer was actually made—and not just for the Miami game—to give him all the time he needed.

But he reacted just the opposite and wouldn't have anything to do with it.

THE LESSONS HE'S TAUGHT

I think what defines him is his character as a human being rather than his 359 wins. The boosters get all upset: "How come Bobby didn't beat this team or win by this much?" We keep reminding them that we hire football coaches to win games *and* build character. They are both equal in my book.

Ultimately, you remember him not for a football win but the character he brings to the table. To me, that lasting memory will be bringing the Make-A-Wish kid into the locker room before the Miami game in 2005. Here it is, the biggest game of the year for Coach Bowden, with all the trouble he's had beating Miami. He brought that kid up in front of the team and had a prayer with him and let him run on the field. He was right there behind him. That's vintage Bobby Bowden.

Probably the best lesson he taught all of us who played for him is that you're going to meet the same people going down that you met going up. And how you treated them going up is how they will treat you coming down. From the time we came in as players, he would take us to church camps, and he would bring kids to practice. He was always doing that.

"Get your priorities straight," he'd say. I can remember him talking to us players about priorities—God, family, and football. And in February of 2006, when we went to that Seminole banquet, it was the same speech and message.

I swear I could shut my eyes and it was 1963 all over again.

RON SIMMONS

THE FIRST ALL-AMERICAN

Ron Simmons was unlike anything Florida State football fans had ever seen. He bench pressed 525 pounds and ran the 40-yard dash in 4.56 seconds. The 6-foot, 235-pounder from Warner Robins, Georgia, possessed the athletic ability to change a game and a football program. And he did both. His impact at Florida State was immediate. He blocked a punt in his first game at FSU in 1977. Simmons had 19 tackles in a 24–3 win over Auburn and again against North Texas State. Sports Illustrated named him the national defensive player of the week after the North Texas State game in which he also made five sacks. He earned freshman All-America honors, and before his career was over, he became the first Seminole to earn consensus All-America honors twice and Bowden's first All-American at Florida State.

Simmons' eligibility had already expired when his name surfaced in the first off-the-field incident to rock Bobby Bowden's program. Simmons was among a group charged with taking televisions from the Maas Brothers department store. Although no longer on the team, Simmons quickly had to face Bowden on the matter. It was the rare time that Simmons had disappointed his coach.

Simmons first made Bowden's day when he selected FSU over Georgia and Auburn. From there it was one highlight after another until injuries, the only opponent that could ever get the better of Simmons, won the final battle. Simmons, because of injury, watched the final 30 minutes of his college career on the bench as Oklahoma beat No. 2 FSU 18–17 in the Orange Bowl following the 1980 season.

Simmons played two years in the United States Football League with the Tampa Bay Bandits, where he rejoined former teammate Jimmy Jordan. But it was in professional wrestling where Simmons became a star before retiring in 2002.

Growing up where I did in South Georgia, I could only be one thing—a Georgia Bulldog. I never even considered Florida State when I first started being recruited in high school. I probably knew more about Bobby Bowden than did Florida State. A friend of the family that I had known as a kid had played for Coach Bowden in college. I had heard of the University of Florida, but Florida State wasn't one of those football schools people talked about when I was in high school.

I just didn't see myself going there. But Gene McDowell, who was coaching linebackers at Florida State, recruited me pretty hard. And in high school I was a linebacker. I got to thinking that Florida State was where I was going to go.

About that time I heard rumors that Coach Bowden was going to leave Florida State. It was on television that Coach Bowden was going to the University of Mississippi. It wasn't true, but I didn't know that at the time. I heard later that another school had told the sports guy to put that out there.

Anyway, when I heard those rumors, I told Gene McDowell, "Look, maybe I need to give this some more consideration." Gene McDowell called Coach Bowden that night and said, "You better come up to Warner Robins and reassure him or let him know whatever it is you are going to do." I'm not sure if even Gene knew what was really happening. That television report was pretty convincing.

Coach Bowden came right up to Warner Robins to assure me that he was going to stay. That was the circumstance of one of my first meetings with Coach Bowden. I think my first questions to him were, "Are you going to stay at Florida State?" and, "Are you serious about that?"

He told me that he wasn't going anywhere—he was staying at Florida State, and he wanted me to be part of his plans for football there.

Ron Simmons provided Bobby Bowden with the foundation to help rebuild Florida State football in the late 1970s. *Photo by Mike Ewen*

Up to then, all of my recruiting had been done by Gene McDowell. But I learned that Coach Bowden was a man of his word. The way he handled the rumors made me want to get to know him more. I knew I wouldn't ever have to question anything he told my family or me. With my background, things had been very hard on me growing up, and I wasn't very impressionable. I had seen everything when it came to life. I didn't need people telling me lies or making me promises that couldn't be kept. When he talked to me, I just knew he was telling it to me straight.

He was genuine and real about my opportunity at Florida State. Looking back, that's something I really appreciated. I had done all these things in high school, but he never promised me the world. He never told me I'd start right away or I would do this or do that. He did promise me this: if I played like I did in high school and worked hard like I did in high school, I would get a good shot of playing my first year. Nobody else told me that. So many coaches make the mistake of promising the world. That's where they get in trouble with a player. I heard a lot of promises from the other coaches that I could start. But all Coach Bowden told me was, "Live up to what you did in the past, and I promise this: you will have an opportunity to play."

He made it clear that whether that would happen was up to me. It's not something he gave me or gave anybody else. We had to earn it. I ended up starting, but he never made any guarantees that I would. He told me exactly what I faced—who was ahead of me, what year he was, how good he was. Nobody else did that with me, but that's what I wanted to know, and I wanted a coach to be honest with me about it, to tell me the truth.

That rumor about him leaving was just part of how crazy the recruiting was. There was a time when Jim Carlen of South Carolina, Vince Dooley of Georgia, and Coach Bowden were all in our house eating dinner. I wish I had a picture of it. Jimmy Womack, who was my stepbrother and went on to be the blocking fullback for Herschel Walker; James Brooks, who went to Auburn; and I were all there at the same time. To see the coaches at that table eating a South Georgian meal of syrup and pork rind skins was fantastic. That told me a lot about Coach Bowden then too. He seemed very comfortable.

The coaches talked about old times. Florida State's program was a lot different than Georgia's at the time, and Auburn had a very good program. These schools had a lot of tradition. They had done a lot of things. They went to bowl games all the time. Florida State hadn't done much of that.

Coach Bowden had just finished his first year there, and really all he could tell me was that he was trying to build something from the ground level up. He couldn't promise what the future would be for Florida State, but he gave me his outlook and what he had in mind for the program. Coach Bowden talked about the kind of player he wanted and the work it would take. He didn't hide anything, but he was positive and said he believed we could do good things, probably like any coach would have said in his position.

When I got down to Tallahassee and started practice, the first thing that struck me was, "Where was the sweet, nice guy? What happened to him?" I looked around and saw the look of the other guys, and I knew I wasn't the only one who thought that. He was working us unbelievably and unrelentingly. At that time, I was thinking, "Wait a minute. What is going on? I was a standout in high school. I shouldn't have to go through this."

But it wasn't that way with Coach Bowden. I was not Ron Simmons from Warner Robins, Georgia, who was a high school All-American. I was just one of a team. Everybody would work the same way—no exceptions, no special treatment. Coach let us know that right away.

He never showed me any favors, even later in my career. I could throw that All-America thing up in front of him, and it didn't mean a thing to him. I didn't get out of doing anything. If I came in after curfew, I was disciplined just like the other guys. I was always glad he was that way.

The message I received that first day was "You are going to work for whatever you get." Among my freshman class, I think we may have had eight guys leave. You have to understand what a tough situation it must have been for a coach to take over—it was once an all-girls school, and the football program had not been doing well before he took over. I remember thinking at the time that he probably had to make a point, but 10 gassers after practice? A gasser was three football fields you had to run around. Come on. It was very intense.

I look at the practices the guys have now, and they have it made. But that hard work had a lot to do with the things we did in 1977, and in the seasons after that, Coach Bowden made sure that we understood we were part of a team. He was smart, and he played on the fact that we were underdogs.

Everybody wanted us for homecoming. We knew that; that was no secret. But Coach Bowden believed in us, and we in turn believed in what the coaches were doing to prepare us. Who would have ever believed we would win 11 games in the 1979 season or go to the Orange Bowl? And even when we did, nobody believed. Everybody thought it was a fluke. And Coach Bowden used that some to motivate us. He was a very good motivator.

He kept what he told us before a game pretty basic: "Play how you've been coached and play with your teammates. Do your job. Don't try to do theirs. You win when you do that."

In certain situations, he would say something about us not getting the respect. But of course, he didn't have to say much about us being underdogs. Usually the opponents' fans, and sometime the opposing players, would take care of that for him. Florida thought they were going to beat us my first year. We were ranked, and they were not, and still I don't think they took us seriously. Their fans didn't. But we won, and I remember the silence and the looks on their fans' faces. That's something that will always be etched in my memory. But Coach Bowden had us prepared. We were well-conditioned and well-disciplined. We played with what we had, and we played with heart. To me, that is one of Coach Bowden's great attributes, at least in my time: the ability to get the most out of what he had. That was a strength.

Even when we started winning a lot of games, I think we still had the attitude of an underdog. We just liked seeing the look on those fans after a game too much. They were sitting there because they couldn't believe the game was over. It was that way when we went to Nebraska in 1980 and beat them—number three in the country. Nobody beat Nebraska at home, and they didn't think the game was over. They were sitting in the stands. They wanted a fifth quarter.

I remember going to one school, and they were calling us "beach bums" and "sissy all-girls school." They had guys on that offensive line that must have been 6-foot-8 and were going to play in the NFL, but they never saw a bunch of guys who could run all day long. They never saw a team like us. And that's where all that work paid off for us. Don't get me wrong. We had some talented guys, but a lot of times we went against teams that had more talent. Coach Bowden's message to us was, "Find a way to win. Nobody's going to outwork us. Nobody." It was that simple.

And we had guys who really loved to play. None of us were thinking about professional football. We just loved to play, and I think that showed. That was the way Coach Bowden was—we could tell. He loves to coach the game.

I didn't have my father around growing up. Coach Bowden took on that role for me and, I think, for a lot of the young men who have come through the program. When I got to Florida State, I learned he was somebody I could go to. I didn't do that very often—just when I needed to. He had a way of saying the things that needed to be said. After the Maas Brothers incident, when I was already through playing, Coach Bowden had me come into his office; you are always on the team with Coach Bowden. It was a mistake I made. He told me to own up to it and move past it. It was a fatherly conversation.

People are always asking me what makes him a great coach. I would answer it the way I have heard a lot of his players put it. What makes him a great coach probably aren't the Xs and Os. It's not the great plays he has drawn up or, as was the case when I was playing, the many upsets that he pulled off. It's the qualities he showed when I first met him. He is genuine and a man of his word. If he weren't, I would have never stepped foot on that Florida State campus.

I'm glad I did. In my travels as a professional wrestler, I have gone to university towns where I could have played, and I think, "How would I have fared if I had played at that university?" I always come up with the same conclusion: thank God that Coach Bowden came up to Warner Robins and said to me, "I'm not going anywhere."

JIMMY JORDAN & WALLY WOODHAM

THE TWO-HEADED QUARTERBACK

JIMMY JORDAN

Jimmy Jordan found out he was going to become the first Florida State athlete to grace the cover of Sports Illustrated while still in school the way he learned about most things. There wasn't much warning or discussion. He was just told to show up at a certain room and a photographer would take his picture. That was that. And on the cover of the November 12, 1979, Sports Illustrated issue, Jordan joined Nebraska's Jarvis Redwine and Ohio State's Art Schlichter and others as the featured players under the headline "WHO'S REALLY NO. 1?"

The way Jordan recalls it, because he was picked to represent FSU, Wally Woodham was named one of FSU's permanent captains for the 1979 team. That team was FSU's first to finish the regular season undefeated.

The core of FSU's success that season was defensive stalwart Ron Simmons and a two-headed quarterback that a Sports Illustrated writer dubbed Wally Jim Jordham. The two Tallahassee Leon High graduates were separated by one grade, but Woodham took a redshirt year at FSU. The two finished their Florida State careers as interchangeable parts, and the quarterback switch usually came without a moment's notice during a game. In FSU's 1977 victory over Florida, the first against the Gators for Bobby Bowden, Woodham gave FSU a 10–3 lead. But when Bowden switched to Jordan, the Seminoles poured it on to finish with a 37–9 win.

Jordan finished with 4,144 passing yards, and Woodham was good for 3,550. Wally Jim Jordham passed for more than 7,600 yards and 61 touchdown passes.

For Wally Woodham and me, starting with that 1979 season, it was almost like we were one person. We took the exact same snaps—whether Wally was starting or it was me. And you just never knew if it was your time. I always remember when I stepped off the bus before the 1980 Orange Bowl to go to the locker room, and Coach Bowden said, "Jimmy, you're starting."

That might have been on purpose on Coach Bowden's part. It was like in our meetings, there was never a lot of attention on me, and not much on Wally, or vice versa. It was always the same. When I got a question, he got a question. If you had taken my statistics and his statistics and put them into one, they would probably still be records. Whoever went in to relieve, it always seemed to work.

But it's a tough thing to do. We were lucky. We were fortunate because it was the times. We didn't care who played as long as we won. It was stressed so much by Coach to win a football game. "I don't care what your stats are. I don't care if you throw five interceptions and one touchdown but we win. If Wally's in there and we win, fine. If Jimmy's in there, fine. If both of you are playing, fine."

There were hard times. Personally, it hurt me tremendously as far as my career down the road because the scouts could not understand why I couldn't beat Wally out. We had a lot of scouts come in here. My arm was pretty strong, so they were really talking to me about the Senior Bowl and my future.

They'd say, "Why can't you beat him out?"

Well, here's why I couldn't beat him out. If I threw an interception, I'd be on the bench. If he threw an interception, he'd probably go to the bench.

I can remember distinctly how difficult it was, especially the closer I got to my senior year. Because it was my senior year, I was getting restless. It's just human nature when NFL scouts are talking to you and saying, "You're going to be one of the top four quarterbacks picked." That's what you're fighting.

How hard is it when you want to play and the other quarterback is taking your team up and down the field, scoring touchdowns, and winning? How many times do you see a quarterback throw two interceptions in the first half, and win the football game in the second half? You dig yourself out. Well, we never got that opportunity. Coach Bowden was telling the press, "I'm going with the pitcher with the hot hand—the fastballer, the curveballer."

The media loved that because it was something to write about. I never remember Coach Bowden ever coming to me and saying, "Jimmy, what do you think about this situation?" He wasn't going to give me that opportunity. We didn't have a choice. That's the way it was. Live with it.

Good thing Wally and I got along. We went out together. We'd bird-hunt together. But we weren't best friends. Sometimes I can't believe it worked. Don't get me wrong—it worked out great for the university. It worked out good for Wally and me; we got a lot of good stuff out of it.

Coach Bowden handled it unbelievably well. You can imagine two kids at that age, both of them want to play. We were from the same high school. This is why I think it worked: Wally and I accepted it, and we said, "This is the way it's going to be." And then *Sports Illustrated* picked up on the two-headed quarterback thing. And then the university started getting publicity.

MEET THE NEW COACH

I was first recruited by Darrell Mudra, and then FSU made a change. People over there asked my mom and dad to come out and meet the new coach at Florida State, Bobby Bowden. Florida State had won one game in the previous two years. I was a big Auburn fan. I loved Pat Sullivan and Terry Beasley. Wally was a big Gator. He liked John Reaves.

I just wasn't a huge Florida State fan at that time. Florida State just wasn't that big in Tallahassee at that time—because they were losing, I guess. I didn't have any ties with FSU. There weren't a lot of people jumping to go to Florida State.

Jimmy Jordan (L) and Wally Woodham were tabbed by a *Sports Illustrated* writer as Wally Jim Jordham and gave Bobby Bowden interchangeable quarterbacks who helped FSU to an undefeated regular season in 1979.
Courtesy of FSU Sports Information

So we went and met Coach Bowden and had dinner with him. Coach Bowden said, "Well, this is what we are going to do. We're going to throw the ball all over the place."

We had heard that he was coming in and was going to run the Veer offense. That was what Florida was running. I was so slow that the linemen outran me. I was really concerned about that, but we got that straight, or at least he told us that we were going to throw the football. And he said he was going to recruit that way: find linemen that could pass block. He was going to run out of the pro set—put two or three receivers out there. And that's basically what he did.

The first thing I thought that night was, "Oh my gosh. This man is a disciplinarian. He's going to change some stuff out there." We had always heard the guys that had been at Florida State a few years before us were a little lackadaisical as far as discipline. I knew right when I talked with him, that playing for him was going to be a job. It was going to be tough the first year or so. And Coach Bowden told me that the first time we met.

I was coming out of Leon with Coach Gene Cox, and I was in the best shape of my life. I thought, "I can handle this." The first day we put pads on, Coach Bowden was in the mat room down there. He backed up in a corner and stood up on a chair and had all of us out in front of him. He said, "Men, I hope you all are ready for this. If I see any hair sticking out of your helmet, I'm cutting it myself. So go to the barber shop tonight."

We're all thinking, "But Coach, there are no barbershops open." This was on a Sunday night before a Monday practice. Of course, we freshmen had no hair—it was already shaved—and we were like, "Let's go."

Some guys had Fu Manchus and stuff, and Coach Bowden said, "There will not be anything on your lip—period." He went on to say, "When we get out there today, you're going to understand what we're going to try and do here. We're not going to lose football games here. That's not going to be acceptable."

I just remember how stern he was about the hair and about not losing football games. And when we got out there the next morning, he circled us up and started doing grass drills.

He would blow his whistle and we would hit the ground, jump up, and hit it again until about 10 people were left standing. That was the first day.

He called us up, the ones that could get up, and said, "Men, now we're going to start practice," and we were like, "Holy cow!"

And for two days it never got outside of seven yards. If you were a quarterback, if you were a kicker, you carried the ball. You ran through those cones, and there were three people waiting for you.

You have to realize, we didn't win but four football games in the three years before Coach Bowden arrived. He went to Florida State and won five the first year. By the time I was a senior, which was only a matter of four years, we were undefeated and playing Oklahoma in the Orange Bowl. And we beat Florida three out of four years.

And it went back to that very first day.

It was a lot like *The Junction Boys*—the way Bear Bryant ran his preseason camp. I watched that movie, and it was scary like that. I remember we'd get little cups of water. Now they're out there with garden hoses. It wasn't barbaric or anything like that, but it was hard-nosed football.

It wasn't any of this wearing shorts the first day. You were throwing up, and then you were practicing. And you did the same thing—you just hit, hit, hit, hit, hit. His staff had that mentality: Gene McDowell, Jim Gladden, Jack Stanton, people like that. They were from the old school. They were coaching football in the Bear Bryant days. I just remember how hard it was.

There was a tendency to go to the younger guys. I think there were two or three senior quarterbacks, and I played as a freshman. Those guys didn't even get to play. They didn't even get on the field. Basically, when something happened to Jimmy Black my freshman year, and I would go in, Coach wouldn't even look at anybody but me. I played a lot as a freshman.

We were at Oklahoma, and Coach Bowden decided, "Guys, this is what we're going to do. We're going to make a youth movement, and I hope it works. So you all better play hard." In my sophomore year, Florida had 11 players drafted in the National Football League. We had players such as Mike Good, who didn't really get recruited. We didn't have guys who were drafted, and we beat them. Now you tell me how that works. That's all heart. That's not ability.

George Haffner was our offensive coordinator, but if Coach Bowden thought he saw something that needed coaching at the quarterback position, he would take care of that himself. He was more of a motivator—getting you ready to play on Saturday, getting the game plan ready—probably more then than he is now with the game plan. At practice he was really into everything. He wanted to touch everything. He was watching the kicking game. I remember him over there with the stopwatch. He went from station to station.

I think Coach Bowden was really heavy into recruiting. I think he did a lot more recruiting than we would ever know about. I think it is amazing how you can take a program from one win in two seasons to undefeated in the fourth year.

The one thing that I think I will remember more than anything about him is that he hated to lose. You didn't want to be around him when we lost.

JUST WALLY, JIMMY, AND BOBBY

On the nights before home games, everybody who was going to dress would be bussed up to Thomasville. The idea was to get us out of town.

Coach Bowden would give us a little pep talk, and then Wally Woodham and I would go to his hotel room for final preparation for the game. It was so funny. We'd go in there, and Coach would already be down to his boxers. He'd have the projector set up, and Wally and I would sit there on the edge of the bed. He'd open up his little briefcase with a brand-new can of Red Man chewing tobacco right there. Then he had his little trash can with a liner so he could spit, and he'd say, "All right, here's what we're going to do."

He'd do this every single game. It didn't matter where we were at—home or away. We'd sit there an hour. Sometimes it might be less, sometimes it might be more. We'd go through a roll of game tape. It was more of "let's look at our opponent play one more time." It was more of a teacher–student but not question and answer. Some coaches I had later on in my career, boy, they would grill you. They would get up on the board with a marker, and they would be that way right up to the night before the game. That's the way they taught. Coach Bowden, at the time, he just wanted you to look at their defense and see what their tendencies were. It was kind of relaxed.

I'll never forget it.

WALLY WOODHAM

Wally Woodham admits it was difficult at times to share quarterback duty with his friend and former Leon High teammate, Jimmy Jordan. But shared playing time didn't keep Woodham out of the record book. He still ranks 12th at FSU both in career yardage (3,469) and career completions (273). He led FSU in his sophomore season with 1,270 yards.

You don't go into Coach Bowden's office unless you have something serious to talk about. I wasn't the type. I'm a pretty serious guy. I'm not going to go into any coach's office to talk about problems unless it's pretty serious. I'm just not that open, but I did go talk to Coach Bowden about my second year. Entering that year, I didn't think I had it. I was ready to quit. I didn't think I could play on the college level. I had gotten down—all that stuff.

I was tired. Football was wearing on me, and it wasn't fun. I wanted to be a student—chill out, drink some beer.

I went and talked to my dad first—that was a big step. I didn't know what he was going to say to me, quite frankly. We hadn't talked about feelings before, so I didn't know if he was going to go crazy. I didn't know what he was going to do.

He said, "Son, if that's what you want to do, quit. You can."

The next step was to go tell Coach Bowden that I thought I was done. I went in there very, very, very nervous. I wasn't sure what I wanted to do. I told him I didn't think I could play football at that level, and he listened to me. Then he told me about all his sons. His oldest son, Steve, didn't play ball, and that was OK with him.

He said, "If playing football is not what you want to do, that's OK. I just don't want you to make a snap decision."

I told him I had already told my dad I was quitting, and that that's what I was going to do, go be a college student. I was in a fraternity. I enjoyed that more. I was tired of all the football. I just wanted go be a regular student. I had it all worked out.

Coach Bowden listened to me for a long time—an hour and a half or more—and that meant a lot. He was like a father. He had more influence on me than anybody other than my dad. Later, I wrote him a letter and told him that he meant so much. The respect I have for him, the way he lived his life—I model that in the way I try to live my life today at 49. He's still a guy I look back to.

He counseled me—only I didn't have to pay $120 an hour. He let me talk. He knew I was pouring my guts out. I was traumatized over this stuff. It was like, "What are the people in Tallahassee going to say? You can imagine the people at the gas station. 'What do you mean, you quit?'"

He asked, "Why don't you take the scout team?"

I said to myself, "Well, dang, I thought I was out of here."

He said, "I just don't want you to make a quick decision—think about it." And I think I left and kind of thought about it. I said to myself that I would get with the scout team, take a redshirt, and get back in shape. I redshirted in '76, Coach Bowden's first year.

I thought, "I'll just hang out, see what happens, and maybe get through the season." I knew it was going to be painful because I knew Jimmy was going to be good. Oh my God. I had played with him before. I said to myself, "Well, just get through the season, and then try to get in shape." I was out of shape. I was going to give it one more shot. No pressure. And I got in better shape. I used to win that 12-minute run that began preseason camp.

Competing for a job like that as a quarterback was tough—both of us coming from Leon. The fact is that Leon High was bigger than anybody at the time.

I COULD READ DISCIPLINE ON HIM THE FIRST TIME HE SPOKE

You have to remember we were at the bottom. First of all, the players were more humble. Today you've got the tops in the country, the blue-chippers. A lot of us were Florida rejects, not your frontline guys. You didn't quite have that ego, that facade. We just came in to be a part of a team. It's changed a little bit, but the way football was played back then was the old Vince Lombardi deal. Gene Cox used to use those old Lombardi sayings, and they brainwash you.

Coach Bowden was the typical football coach—short-cut, tight hair. I could read discipline on him the first time he spoke to us. There were going to be some changes. It felt right because some of the talent was already there. It felt good. I came from Leon High School. It felt right.

Coach Bowden was firm, yet he'd talk to you. I said to myself, "He's serious." He probably did a lot more hands-on then than I guess he does now. Discipline was a big part of his deal.

Coach Bowden would go over the games he thought we could win. He tried to get people to believe we could win a certain number, but he wasn't unrealistic. He said, "You're not going to win them all." But he would go through and try to get people to believe in what we could do. And then I think too, with individuals, he'd work with them on the side and try to let them know that they could be all that they could be. He let them be the best they could be. Again, I think he knew he had a base of kids he could win with.

The message I took from him is "We are going to get this thing done. We are going to play as one. If you can't play as one, you probably don't need to be here. We are going to lock up, and we are going to win and lose together."

Coach Bowden was enthusiastic and firm, but also positive. That was the good thing about Coach Bowden. Coach would encourage you. Defensive coaches, a lot of times they would kind of be negative. Coach Bowden would encourage you yet push you.

I remember one time he called me out. He got the point across: he would do what it took. It was 1978—our 8-3 year. We played Mississippi State out there. I had hurt my shoulder the game before, so Jimmy started the game. We were getting waxed—beat pretty good. The coaches asked me, "Could you go in?" and I said no. Mississippi State beat us 55–27.

When we got back into the quarterbacks-only meeting that next week, Coach Bowden came in, and he was really upset. He said, "Wally, I believe Pittsburgh's Matt Cavanaugh would have gone the other day." You see, offensive coordinator George Haffner had come to FSU from Pitt. So by saying that right there in front of all those guys, he shamed me. It was a good thing. He got my attention and said, "I don't believe you gave me what I needed."

It quieted me up pretty quick. He did exactly what I would do to my kid if I didn't think things were right. He needed to. We were losing the battle, and he needed somebody to go to war. I didn't go. Football's a miniwar. You want to get your people with you. If they're not going to get with you, you want them to get the hell out of there. That's being honest in the most Christian way I can say it.

I think at that time he was really trying to get things going. He was trying to win as quick as he possibly could. In '77, we got those 10 wins and really got going good. I think he was trying to find the right combination.

It didn't start out with Jimmy and me switching off in games in '77. By '78 and '79, that changed. I think Coach was just trying to keep winning. I think another thing that influenced Coach's decision to use two quarterbacks was that he was new here. I don't think it was the main thing, but he knew we were two Tallahassee boys from Leon High School. Back then, you didn't mess with Leon High School. If I were Coach, and I had two Leon High School guys, and I knew there were a lot of people watching Leon High School football, I'd make sure both of those guys got a shot.

But the only reason he pulled us out during games was because we weren't doing our jobs on the field. In my junior year, I started realizing that was just part of it. I didn't like it, but that was part of it. We had to be ready. He could tell when a player was intimidated. He had a good feel for when to make a switch.

Coach Bowden could communicate. He had a way that he could chum up with you a bit, and he's still got it today. He conveyed that in the Tangerine Bowl. He said, "You're still my man"—something to that effect that made me feel good.

ELVIS PRESLEY DIED TODAY

The thing that comes to mind for me when I think about that time in my life is Coach Bowden's faith. The greatest gift he gave me probably was faith in God.

I remember one day he called us around—you know, college guys, young guys, all in shape. Good-looking, strong guys. We thought we were somebody. Coach Bowden reminded us of what was most important in life. I remember he said, "Elvis Presley died today. I hope he knows where he's going."

He talked to us about morality too. Women were a big part of the deal. I remember another time he said, "There's been talk of a lot of ladies staying up in the dorms with the men. And one day that could be your daughter."

So he wasn't real preachy, and that meant a lot to me.

He can sit around, shoot the breeze, cut the jive, and talk the trash with you. Athletes like that, and he can do it. He's down-home; he's Southern; and he believes in discipline. He's a Christian. What else do you want in the South?

That's why he came here. That's why he fits here. That's why he made it.

MONK BONASORTE

◄ ● ❯❯❯❯❯❯ ○ ❮❮❮❮❮❮ ● ►

THE WALK-ON

Monk Bonasorte walked on to the Florida State football team in 1977 as an unknown. He walked away as a future FSU Hall of Fame member after grabbing 15 career interceptions. Twenty-six years later, it is a feat that still ranks second among all Seminoles. Bonasorte earned third-team Associated Press All-America honors in 1979 as a safety and was named a second-team All-America by Football News *in 1980. Bonasorte participated in two Orange Bowls and earned first-team All–South Independent honors in 1980.*

But Bonasorte also assured himself of being known by future FSU football players as the Seminole who Bobby Bowden often mentions in motivational speeches about overcoming long odds and working hard.

Since returning to Florida State and becoming the executive director of the FSU Varsity Club, Bonasorte has become the strongest tie between Florida State and its former football players. Under his leadership, the Varsity Club has completed a stadium box for FSU lettermen in all sports.

Nobody at Florida State knew me when I first arrived in Tallahassee as a walk-on during the spring of 1977. I didn't have any film to show coaches from my high school days in Homestead, Pennsylvania, a steel mill town near Pittsburgh. I weighed 210 pounds, and I had been a tight end and defensive end back in high school.

The only tie I had to Florida State, if you can even call it that, was that I had an old friend and coach who had called Florida State defensive coordinator Jack Stanton about me. I think this friend just wore

Jack Stanton out with his phone calls. Finally, Coach Stanton told me to come on down to Tallahassee. I wasn't even an invited walk-on.

I had been out of high school for two years. At that time I played recreational football in what was known as the beer league. It was called that because the sidelines were littered with broken beer bottles. All I cared to do was be on the corner drinking beer and be a homeboy. That's what we did. I was drinking beer at an early age.

Florida State was on a trimester system at that time, and I arrived in March. Two of my buddies went down there with me. The week after I got down there, one of my best friends back home was stabbed in a bar and killed. I was glad I had gotten out of there.

Even though I had played defensive end in high school, that spring I was fifth or sixth on the depth chart at safety. I had never played that position before. During spring practice, I recovered a fumble and ran it back 98 yards. I also made an interception. Coach Bowden saw that I was making plays. But at the end of spring practice, he came up to me and said, "Monk, I like you, but I cannot offer you a scholarship."

Coach had a lot of new guys coming in the fall. This was his first real recruiting class at Florida State. I understood. He was under pressure. In his first year at Florida State he was 5-6, and he didn't want to take chances on a walk-on he had never seen play during a season. But I needed a scholarship, because I had cashed in an insurance policy to pay my way through school that spring. I couldn't afford to come back to Florida State in the fall paying my own way.

Coach Bowden said, "I'll tell you what I will do. We'll bring you back in for two-a-days, and we'll see what happens after two-a-days."

There were no guarantees, but I felt strongly that I had to at least try. The chance for something better was at Florida State and in Tallahassee, not back in Pittsburgh. The steel mills were closing, and a lot of my friends had lost their jobs and had to live with their parents. There didn't seem to be any other way I could get out of a ghetto-type environment, which is really what I had lived in.

Coach Bowden never promised anything, and I think that is something people will tell you about him. Coach Bowden will tell you how

Monk Bonasorte earned a place in FSU football lore and Bobby Bowden's heart for beating all odds as a walk-on to become a starter.
Courtesy of FSU Sports Information

it is. He doesn't promise you something that he can't deliver. From a player's standpoint, that is a really important quality for a coach.

At the end of two-a-days, Coach Bowden offered me a scholarship. And it wasn't all because of what I did. Some people got hurt, and I was at the right place at the right time. It was the beginning of a feeling that something really good could happen down there.

I like the label *overachiever*—especially now with the program reaching the level it has since my playing days in signing all these great high school athletes who can run the 40-yard dash in 4.3 seconds. When the NFL scouts came to test us, I ran the 40-yard dash in 5.0 seconds. Yet I was able to make Florida State's Hall of Fame. I had to work a lot harder. Coach Bowden is like any coach; he wants the most talented players he can find, and Coach has brought in a bunch of great athletes. But I think Coach Bowden also has a special place or admiration for players who overachieve. He has had a bunch of them throughout his career at FSU who have helped make the program a winner.

A GREAT MOTIVATOR

Coach Bowden was big on goal-setting. We, the players, would have to listen to these Grant Teaff motivational-type tapes on topics like goal-setting almost every day.

When I was a sophomore, I had reconstructive knee surgery, and one of the doctors said that I would probably not play again—as slow as I already was. When I went home, I listened to those tapes all summer. One of the steps was to write your goals on a piece of paper and stick them on your mirror. Every day as I shaved, I read those goals and thought about how I was going to accomplish them. I decided I was going to work out two hours a day on lifts with my legs and do these different drills, such as backpedaling. My goal in my junior year at Florida State was to lead the nation in interceptions, be an All-American, and set school records. That junior season I lead the nation in interceptions up to the last game of the year, set two records at Florida State, and was a third-team All-American. That goal-setting worked. But I had to work at it. That was something Coach Bowden always stressed—work hard.

He had a great way of motivating us. Even when we were behind, he just knew what to do and which personnel to put in. You would really see that with quarterbacks Jimmy Jordan and Wally Woodham. That was something to watch—Coach knowing the right time to put one of them into the game.

When it came to motivating us, he wouldn't have to say much. He would tell us—"Defense, if they don't score, you win." It was simple, but it motivated us. He did it without yelling at us. I've seen some coaches berate the players and jump all over them. Coach Bowden would say two or three things, and that would be enough. We respected him, and he respected us.

He didn't panic, and that reflected upon his personality. At Nebraska in 1980, we were behind, and they were moving the ball. Nebraska was ranked third in the country, and we had never defeated a team ranked that high. We went into halftime behind 14–3. Coach Bowden didn't panic. He was calm with us. There were times he would get excited, but I never saw him go over the top and get into a guy's face.

He told us what we needed to do, and he made the point that we were as good as they were. We were in a hostile environment, and he said we were handling it well. We won the game 18–14. Coach Bowden still considers it to be one of his biggest wins at Florida State.

And the thing is we had lost to Miami 10–9 the week before. That was a game we should have won. Miami threw the ball out of the end zone. In our opinion, that pass was not catchable, but the officials called pass interference on Gary Henry. They put the ball on the 1-yard line after the penalty, and that's how they got ahead.

We were dejected after the game and into the next week. But Coach Bowden had us ready for this big game at Nebraska. He never questioned or doubted us. Take that Nebraska game; they were beating us pretty good. They were moving the ball, and we weren't. In Coach Bowden we never saw or sensed panic.

And that Miami game told us a lot about Coach Bowden too. We went for a two-point conversion, and he never wavered on that. Players liked that about him. We didn't go for a tie; we came to win the foot-ball game. No one ever second-guessed that decision. Coach played to win.

The next game after the Nebraska win, we were at home against Pittsburgh, and they had all these future NFL players on their team—great players such as Dan Marino and Hugh Green. We neutralized their speed by running right at them. Coach Bowden had convinced us we could pull that off.

During that season, and the whole time I played for Florida State, the expectations were a lot different than they are now. The first year after Coach Bowden was 5-6, we went 10-2 and played in the Tangerine Bowl. Then we went 8-3 and didn't go to a bowl game. Fans loved us at 8-3. We had legions of fans waiting for us at the airport when we arrived home no matter what happened at the game.

There was no reason to be frustrated or feel pressure—not for the players or for the staff or for Coach Bowden. I don't think it is as fun for Coach Bowden anymore. I think the difference now is that the game has changed. It's a business. When I played, it was more of a game. I'm sure he wishes that it was still a game. Now he's criticized by parents. He's criticized by fans. And he's criti-cized more by the media. I think it is hard on him. He's not used to the criticism. Maybe if he were 40 or 50 years old, it would be different.

College football is different in another way for coaches and play-ers. Everything is being watched. We got into trouble, and when we did, the coaches would have us get up and run at five o'clock in the morning. I spent a lot of time at the county line, running back to the campus with some coach driving behind me and my roommates. It was far. If you have kids, and they get in trouble, you don't tell the world. And that's the way it was back then. People are going to mess up, but it's different for Coach Bowden now.

I've seen him frustrated and angry the last couple of years, but I never saw that as a player. It was a different time. We were part of the foundation. We set goals and then worked hard to accomplish them, and we learned that as much as anything from Coach.

After I left Florida State, that kind of left me. But now that I am working again with Coach Bowden, all things he taught me about goal-setting have come back. When I first came back to Tallahassee, my goal was to come back and work at Florida State no matter what had happened.

A PREACHER BUT NOT PREACHY

There is a great saying that goes, "To be old and wise you must first be young and stupid." And there was a time I fit in that young and stupid mold. I was a row-house, inner-city boy from Pittsburgh when I came to Florida State. I had my share of things that happened in my life that I wasn't too proud of, and the one thing that I respected about Coach Bowden is that he never judged me. And I can't overstate how important that quality is, because most people judge each other. Coach does not put himself above anybody. He always makes you feel welcome.

Coach Bowden is a preacher, but he's not preachy. He never put us in a position where he talked at us or talked down to us. He talked to us: "What can we do to correct this or move on to something better?" Here is a coach who has all these people from these diverse backgrounds, and he knew how to deal with us, all of his players. He had this way of molding us into being better people. He did it subtly without throwing all that you did in your past at you.

To me, Coach Bowden is a greater football coach not because of wins and losses but because of what he does for individuals and what he's done for me personally in my life.

I would not be back here at Florida State if not for Coach Bowden. And I'm not sure where I would be in my life if not for Coach Bowden. After I finished school and left Tallahassee, there was a time when I made some mistakes in my life. I put myself in a tough spot.

It was then that Coach sent this letter, which I still have. It is dated January 19, 1998. This is what he wrote:

Dear Monk

I received your letter and it is great to hear from you. Can't wait to see you again.

I love you as much now as I ever did and that is with all I got. I'm so proud of you and your achievements. I just never had a young man to achieve more from the first day he was on my team until the day he left.

Now mistakes that you have made, we all have made in our lives one way or another in the eyes of God. All mistakes are equal, big or small. You have made one and you have paid the price. If I can help you get started again don't hesitate to call me.

Monk, there is something I found out in trying to be a Christian. No. 1, I could never live a life good enough deserving to be saved by Christ. And you are not saved by what you do. You are saved by your faith and belief and trust in Jesus Christ. You can never earn it. Don't try. Just do the best you can.

You are as much loved and as worthy as anybody on earth. I look forward to seeing you again and thank you so much for your letter.

Give my love to your family.

Sincerely,

Coach Bowden

Before I received that, I was thinking, "What do I have to come back to Tallahassee for?" I didn't have a job. There were not a lot of reasons to return to Tallahassee. But when I got the letter from Coach, it kind of made me feel that I could move on and not be embarrassed about it. His message was that my problem was between me and God and that we all make mistakes.

I was concerned about coming back to Tallahassee. Twenty-five years ago it was in the Bible Belt. It was Baptist, and some people were very judgmental. But I decided that if Coach Bowden could accept me back, then I would forge my way through it all. And now I'm in a position with the Varsity Club to work with the man, and it is a pinch-me–like dream.

The positive effect that Coach Bowden has on his players, including me, is often overlooked.

Coach Bowden has a hundred kids he has to deal with, and he is going to have problems he must handle. People criticize him because he's had players not do the right things. And he has also been criticized for how he disciplines those players—his three-strikes rule. If after one mistake, a player is thrown to the wolves, what are his chances in life? I believe if you throw away that person after one mistake, his chances of being successful in life go down the drain.

I don't believe people understand how Coach Bowden subtly and effectively delivers his message and teaches his players. My father taught me about working hard. He had the same job forever and taught me about responsibility—he paid his bills on time. But Coach Bowden demonstrated other qualities. He cares about his players—even after they leave. Even before my job with the Varsity Club, he would ask me to bring to his office any former players who come around so he could see them. I don't know how many other coaches do that. I've been around other coaches. My brother played for Pittsburgh.

A lot of coaches are just there for the moment.

Coach Bowden does have a concern and a care. He asks how his former players are doing, and if any are in trouble, he reaches out to them. Coach has taught me about dealing with people and about dealing with situations more than I ever learned when I was young. I was a street person.

I didn't realize how important Coach Bowden is while I was here, and I didn't realize that right after I left. But as I grew older and had a family, I really began to understand what he had meant and what he had taught me.

I came to understand what Kenny Stabler and Joe Namath used to say when I was younger. They never said they played for Alabama. They said they played for Bear Bryant. And after playing at Florida State, I knew what that meant. We played for Bobby Bowden. We gave our all for him.

When I go back to Pittsburgh, my friends always want to ask about Bobby Bowden. It's during those times I understand how people look at him. To me, he is still Coach, and he is my friend.

Maybe it will all hit me when Coach Bowden leaves. And when he does, Florida State won't be the same. To have Coach in your life is to know that if you need something or need him, he is there. You don't have to go through hoops and three days of calling him.

It hurts me that he receives all this criticism for losing four or five games when you consider what he has done for kids' lives. People are so worried about wins and losses. I think you measure Coach Bowden by what he has done for his players and seeing where they are today. Take someone with my background—and where I grew up in Pittsburgh—and you appreciate the importance of that.

There's that saying, "If you can save one kid's life. . . ." Well, he saved mine.

JAMIE DUKES & SAMMIE SMITH

—◄◆►◯◄◆►—

THE ROOMMATES

Nothing kept Jamie Dukes from being a starter during his four-year career at Florida State—neither the big-bodied defensive linemen who pounded the 1985 consensus All-America guard and future 11-year NFL standout in practices nor those in the 48 consecutive games he started for the Seminoles. Entering the 2006 season, Dukes remains one of just four offensive linemen in FSU history to start every game as a freshman. And in his senior year, Dukes led FSU to a 9-3 record. FSU went 33-13-2 during Dukes' four seasons, but Dukes' play predicted even better days ahead for Bowden and the Seminoles. Dukes' roommate in Burt Reynolds Hall during his senior season was another Central Floridian, a freshman tailback named Sammie Smith, who would sit out that 1985 season. Smith's appearance signaled the beginning of a NCAA-record 14-year stretch of top-5 Associated Press finishes and 10-win seasons.

The cohost of a radio and television show based out of Atlanta, where he played eight years for the Falcons after being snubbed in the NFL Draft, Dukes maintains regular contact with his former coach.

When I arrived at Florida State in 1982, we were more in the process of setting the stage for rebuilding. In 1979 and 1980, the program had gone to the Orange Bowl. After that, we had attrition. In my freshman year, we went 9-3 and made the Gator Bowl. Then we had some drop-off. The 1984 season, when we won just seven games, was probably the toughest time. We then finished with another Gator Bowl and another 9-3 record in my senior year.

We were an independent team then, and Coach Bowden and his teams already had the reputation of being road warriors. That continued with us. We went into Lincoln against Nebraska and won in 1985. We won at Ohio State in 1982.

He motivated by empowering us: "Let's show these guys who you are. They are no better than you are. We've got speed, talent, power, and NFL-caliber players here. We do what we're supposed to offensively."

We were always among the top teams in points scored. Every game was a track meet. And it was during that time things began to change on defense. You could tell what was ahead by the caliber of athlete that was coming in. It was obvious we had gotten some real athletes.

My senior year was the freshman class of Deion Sanders and Sammie Smith. There also were guys like Keith Carter and Eric Hayes, who were highly recruited in that class. Odell Haggins was in that class. That was the biggest recruiting class. You could see great things were about to happen. I remember the first day we got on the field and they paired up and ran 40s. And there was Deion, beating the guy who had won the state championship in the 100-yard dash. They lined up again, and he beat him again. And we were thinking, "Wow."

Coach Bowden had a good eye for talent. The people he had around him when I was there also had a good eye for talent: Bob Harbison, Jim Gladden, Gene McDowell, John Eason, Mickey Andrews, and Chuck Amato. They demanded us to work. That was Coach Bowden's way. That was established before I got there. We were better conditioned than anybody we played because of our mat drills and our conditioning. That happened going back to when Ron Simmons was there. If we got beat, we just got beat. It wasn't that we wilted. The conditioning was one of the reasons we had so many guys go into the NFL. The foundation Coach laid certainly made a difference. And it wasn't just the work we did—stressing special teams and blocking punts, that started with Bobby. Coach Bowden's formula was unseen.

IF YOU GUYS ARE SCARED, WE DON'T HAVE TO GO BACK OUT THERE

From that first season I was around him, he has not changed—not a drop. That's what has been so amazing. I don't recall him changing at all. I've probably seen a different Coach Bowden during the 2005 season more than any other year because of the verbal and written attacks on his son Jeff. For Coach Bowden to have made some of the comments he made, that has been a real shocker to me. And that's the first time I can really honestly say that I have seen Coach Bowden under some measure of pressure. This is the first of any cracks I've seen in Coach Bowden. You just don't see anything get to him.

We lost to Florida every one of my years. Against Florida, I was our player of the game two or three times—as a lineman. That's not good. It's just not good. It ate at him, but in my mind, he never let his frustration get to the point where it reached us—where he took frustration out on us.

He is competitive, but he doesn't put the pressure on others. There's a Tommy Tuberville kind of competitiveness, where a coach might call a player out on the sideline and blast him out. You didn't see that with Bobby. You knew it ate him up to lose, but part of the magic was he didn't translate that into anger or retribution. That doesn't mean if we didn't abide by the rules we weren't going to do extra stadium stairs. No, we were still going to do that.

I've heard Coach Vince Dooley criticize Coach Bowden and disagree with how he disciplined his players. I agree with Coach Bowden wholeheartedly—and I had this bite me as a pro—if you suspend a guy for a game, you hurt the team. If you run that guy until his bowels release, you discipline the player. It's real simple. I would much rather miss a start than have to get up at six o'clock every morning for a week to run stadium steps and then have to run them again after practice. From a fan's perspective, suspension from a game is cute. But the last thing a player wants to go through is the running. Bobby would never punish the team unless it was under certain circumstances. He really had a very unique knack of getting his point across. Yes, he hates to lose. There are some coaches who

I've seen who are vindictive—some are even spiteful to a certain extent. That was something he never was.

He was very positive. At halftime, we would meet with our coaches, and then with a couple of minutes left, he'd talk to us. Of course, he was always taking notes, and he would pull that pad out when he talked to us. I can think of only one game where we just completely melted down and he said something a little stronger than "Dadgummit." That was a time when he was really disappointed in the effort.

Now there were a couple of times he gave us his halftime talk with a kind of sarcasm, a smirk. "Now if you guys are scared, we don't have to go back out there. I'll tell them something."

Very rarely did he not build us up after a loss. He always found a way to help us build for the next game. He would get on us at times if the effort was not there, but very rarely did that happen in the game. If we turned the ball over and did stupid stuff, which we sometimes did, he would quickly point out, "Guys, you are killing us."

He did a good job of being positive and fair. If nothing else, he was always fair. You look at the All-Americans who went into that program, and that had to be a tough thing to manage at times. There was not a time I can recall when politics kept a great player on the bench. If you could play, Coach was going to get you on the field. I always thought that it had to be the toughest job in America to have all these kids continue to come in here—all these high school All-Americans—and have them sit on the bench. But it goes back to him never promising, "You will start if you come here."

He never put himself in a position where he promised somebody he was going to start. I've always been very conscious of that and very respectful of that situation. I have always heard Coach Jimmy Johnson was that kind of guy too. He was going to start the best guy.

WALKED ON WATER

My first impression of Coach Bowden was that he was a good man. My mother loved him because of his walk—his faith that was and still is legendary. She was extremely concerned that I get in the right envi-

Bobby Bowden spotted something special in Jamie Dukes, who began his string of 48 consecutive starts as a true freshman in 1982.
Courtesy of FSU Sports Information

ronment. Bobby couldn't walk on water, but Bobby walked on water to her. And Coach Bowden made sure that I understood the vices out there for college football players and how quickly I could get off-kilter.

Bobby was a coach who drew you in with his passion for the game, his sincerity. He showed you how to live your life with balance. "Don't get too high. Don't get too low"—even though he may have teared up or gussied up one time in front of us after a loss.

The Florida State coaches liked me because I was athletic. I was coming in to play right away. Coach Bowden had a lot of confidence in me, and he did a lot to help my confidence. He was upbeat, but he also let me know how it was. He said, "We are going to give you an opportunity to start, and if you can handle it, you can handle it."

His first concern was to make sure I knew what I was doing. From a guard's standpoint, the offense was pull, pull, pull. I got that part figured out—and the part about having to play hurt.

Coach did have a problem with guys being injured. He understood, but he certainly did not like it. You can't make the club in the tub. I think that was the signature of guys who played for Coach Bowden; they would play every single game, hurt or not—ribs or no ribs. By and large, if you were not working in practice, you would not be able to play. There was that rare exception, but if you were at Florida State, you worked.

We had one year where it seemed to be 100 degrees every day. The one thing that players prayed for during that year's two-a-days was rain. That would be our one day off. With either a thunderstorm or lightning, we wouldn't have to practice. We would always joke and say we knew that Bobby Bowden was on the top of the building, parting the sky.

SAMMIE SMITH

Sammie Smith never enjoyed the All-America accolades heaped on his freshman-year roommate, Jamie Dukes. But the big back with blistering speed did plenty in three seasons to help take Florida State into its dynasty years. During his junior year, he rushed for 1,230 yards—a mark only Warrick Dunn has eclipsed in the history of Florida State football. In 1989, Smith became the first Seminole under Bobby Bowden to skip his final year of eligibility to enter professional football early. The Miami Dolphins picked Smith in the first round with the ninth overall pick.

Smith discussed his decision to leave FSU early with Bowden. After he left FSU, correspondences with his former coach became even more serious. Smith was convicted in 1996 for distribution of cocaine after being caught in a federal sting operation. While serving part of a seven-year sentence, Bowden and his staff corresponded with Smith. Assistant coach Jim Gladden asked Smith in 1998 to tape a video on the importance of making the right decisions. From the Federal Correctional Institute in Edgefield, South Carolina, Smith looked into a camera and simply but poignantly told FSU players: "Think about what you do."

Sammie Smith now lives in Mount Dora, Florida, and owns a business in Orlando.

In my freshman year, my roommate, Jamie Dukes, would express to me that we, the players, had to make something really big happen in the next few years. We had gone to the Gator Bowl in the 1985 season, and he just thought we would have even bigger accomplishments.

I challenged myself at Florida State because I wanted to be part of something that was being turned around. Right away, I knew the football team could be something special. There was a lot of talent just in our recruiting class. And the first thing I noticed about Coach Bowden was that he surrounded himself with people who had the same work ethic and drive that he possessed. The people at Florida State were just an extension of Coach Bowden. The coaches were able to trickle that attitude down to the players.

With each year, you could see how good we could be. We had turned the program around and had been so close to a championship. Honestly, I think some of the teams we had were better than the ones that won the championships. We built a good foundation for other players to want to come to Florida State. We won some big games— especially the bowl games. We beat Nebraska, and in my last game, we beat Auburn in the Sugar Bowl.

Coach Bowden really had a command of what was going on with his program. I don't know what is going on now—it's been over 20 years since I first arrived at Florida State. Coach believed in us, and we believed in him. He wanted to win as bad as we wanted to win.

Against Miami in 1987, we went for the win with a two-point conversion. We could have gone for the tie and probably won a national championship that year. Miami won the game 26–25 when we didn't get the two-point conversion, and Miami won the national championship that year. We finished second after beating Nebraska in the Fiesta Bowl.

We hadn't beaten Miami in a while. Deion Sanders played a brilliant game, and I had 189 yards that day. We fought the whole game. But even with all that, and what happened with the national championship, that was the right thing for Coach Bowden to do. I will always remember us saying to Coach Bowden before that play that we wanted to win; we wanted to go for the win.

It was a crushing loss, and it hurt to lose that game more so than any game I lost in my life. We were ahead 19–3 in the third quarter, and we were pretty much pounding them the whole game. It hurt. It wasn't something we could blame on Coach. We just didn't execute. In fact, we respected Coach Bowden for going for the win and having faith in us.

The only question I can remember having was, "Why wasn't I in the game at the time we went for the two-point conversion?" I had carried the ball 30 times. We faked the run, but I wasn't in the game. I don't know if we didn't have the time to make the decision or what happened. Dexter Carter was in there, and with me not in there after having all those carries, it was like they knew we were going to throw the ball. And we did throw it, and Miami knocked it down.

But even if we didn't agree with all the decisions, guys played hard for Coach Bowden. You could see it in the games that you knew were real important to him. Of course, it didn't take much to hype us up to play Florida, but we also knew how important that game was to him, and we really wanted to win it for him. He had lost six games in a row to Florida before winning in 1987. It was a sore spot for him to lose to those folks every year.

When we did lose a game—and we didn't lose a lot of them— Coach Bowden had a way of making us feel good about ourselves. He made us feel good about the effort that we put out even though inside we were crushed. He was not a sore loser.

Bobby Bowden (L) shares an interview with Sammie Smith prior to the 1989 Sugar Bowl, which FSU won 13–7 over Auburn. *Courtesy of Ryals Lee, FSU Photo Lab*

UNSELFISH ADVICE

Even before the recruiting process began, I had already developed thoughts and opinions of Coach Bowden as a person. Beginning in the ninth grade, I had a chance to go to summer football camps at Florida State. Our high school coach at Apopka would find a way to get a few of the guys to go to different camps and Fellowship of Christian Athlete events.

Coach Bowden might not have known me from any other kid he was recruiting, but I definitely remembered him from those camps. I felt like he was a coach I could come to with anything personal and could get to know him off the field.

Coach was that way during my time at Florida State and even after my career was over. One thing I don't remember talking to him much about were the practices. I hated practice. I had a real fast metabolism and would lose a lot of fluids. And after a lot of games, even back in high school, I would have these real bad cramps. One time in practice during two-a-days, I lost 11 pounds. And then after the second practice, I was down a total of 20 pounds. I came off the field, and I was in a total body cramp. Practices just weren't fun, but that's not something I remember being in conflict with him about.

I felt I could talk to him about anything. When I started thinking about entering the NFL Draft, I went to Coach Bowden. He told me that the decision was mine to make. He understood that I had a wife and a young baby at the time. He even told me that I had a chance to be a first-round pick. He told me, "I want you to stay for your senior year, but I understand if you don't stay."

That conversation showed me that he wasn't selfish and that he cared more about me and providing for my family than he did about winning football games. He thought more of my situation and my opportunity than he did of his opportunity as a coach if I returned.

Then later when I had "the incident," there were a lot of people who were behind me while I was away in prison. That included players such as William Floyd and coaches such as Jim Gladden. And to me, when you get that kind of support from a coach, that's just another extension of Coach Bowden. While I was going through the process, Coach wrote a letter that was sent to my attorney to speak on my behalf. I think of all the players who had something happen and how he kept his belief in them.

The most touching thing was when I was asked to do that video from prison. I know that was an extension of Coach Bowden. It gave me a sense of belonging. Here I was going through one of the toughest times of my life, and it gave me a feeling of being a part of something. That meant something to have a chance to give something back to my school.

I will remember him as a father figure. I really hold him in the highest regard. He would have been successful in anything he had decided to do.

BRAD JOHNSON

⊷⊶⊷─◦─⊷⊶⊷

THE RESILIENT ONE

Brad Johnson didn't fit the mold of a Bobby Bowden–coached quarter-back. The Parade All-American football player, whose first love was basket-ball, stood 6 feet 6 inches. The North Carolinian also possessed an exception-ally strong arm. The two-sport standout's year-round fitness regimen soon became legendary among his teammates and coaches, following his arrival in Tallahassee in 1987. Johnson started the first six games of the 1990 sea-son—his junior year. But in that season's sixth game, Casey Weldon took over for Johnson in the second quarter. Brad Johnson had just one more start as a Seminole—against Louisville his senior season—and that was because of an injury to Weldon, who became the Heisman Trophy runner-up in 1991.

Brad Johnson was selected by Minnesota in the ninth round of the 1992 NFL Draft, and he was the winning quarterback for Tampa Bay in the 2003 Super Bowl. Johnson, who in the NFL off-season lives in Tallahassee, where he is active in community fundraisers and charities—including the Ronald McDonald House—rejoined the Vikings in 2005 and started the final six games.

The 2006 season will be his 15th in the NFL—quite the accomplishment for a quarterback who mostly played backup during his Florida State career.

The great thing about my situation at Florida State was that Coach Bowden still gave me so much room to grow even though I wasn't starting during the end of my junior and then senior year.

He would always play guys back then if we had a lead. As a backup, you were in the game early. There were times when Casey

Weldon was starting as a senior, and he was up for the Heisman Trophy, yet he would be pulled in the second quarter and I would play. Coach Bowden wasn't about running up the score.

Mostly the growth came in practice. Coach Bowden always harped on this, and you still hear guys talk about it: the competition level in practice was going to be much harder than in the games. And it usually was. We were going against Deion Sanders—he was the best one by far. But Terrell Buckley was statistically the best defensive back who played there. To go compete against Deion, Terrell Buckley, LeRoy Butler, or Marvin Jones—that was where we all got good more than anywhere else. I really believe that. Those are the guys I have been going against the past 14 years in the NFL.

Coach Bowden always pushed us to another level, and he always talked about that. Whether it was to be a starter or to win the national championship—we always strived to be better. We played for the national title. That was the bottom line. If we did not win the national championship, we were not successful. That's the way it was. We didn't settle for anything less. We were always working for something more. There wasn't a huge celebration after the Fiesta Bowl or the Cotton Bowl. The week after the bowl, we were in the weight room getting ready for mat drills, getting ready for spring ball. It was always about competition.

Coach Bowden always talked about the great athletes who had gone on to the next level—how hard Jerry Rice would work and what greatness it was going to take to get to the next level. He kind of held the NFL in front of us like a carrot—that's where we wanted to be. And once we got there, we were prepared, and that was because of the competition level. We pushed ourselves from mat drills to practice, and that was especially true for me and Casey Weldon. We were going head to head. We would thrive off of each other. Who could throw the better ball? Who had the better practice? Who could throw the better out-route?

During my time in the NFL, it has always been interesting to see which teams draft players from certain universities. The great players will come out of Florida State, out of the University of Miami, Ohio State, and Southern Cal. There is a mentality about those players and how they are taught. At Tampa Bay, Tony Dungy was big in the

Florida State and Miami types of players. There was a certain kind of mold—the way the practices were run and mat drills were run.

There's something about being part of Coach Bowden's program that carries over to the NFL. You're used to winning. You show up early to meetings with paper and pencil, and you show up early for the bus. There was a toughness about Florida State players, and that reflected what Coach Bowden was all about.

NICE TOSS, BUDDY

The first time I saw Florida State football in person, the team played Oklahoma in the 1980 Orange Bowl. I attended Coach Bowden's camp when I was going into the eighth grade, and I met him on the field. That was the first time I met him. I was a nervous wreck trying to throw spirals. He said something to me like, "Nice toss, buddy."

Florida State, at the time I signed, was a Peach Bowl, All-American Bowl kind of team. They had short quarterbacks there: Danny McManus, Peter Tom Willis, and Chip Ferguson. At that time, the big quarterback in college football was Vinny Testaverde of Miami. He won the Heisman in 1986. He was the No. 1 guy drafted in the 1987 NFL Draft. Coach Bowden's point to me—his selling point—was that the whole next wave would be tall guys like Testaverde. I even wore the same jersey number as Vinny, 14.

Coach Bowden was a great salesman, but I felt like his prediction was true. He had a vision of something. He told me that Casey was a skinny grunt at North Florida Christian and would probably never make it. And he told Casey I would probably go play basketball. They got us.

Coach Bowden actually spoke at my high school banquet. For Owen High, that was huge. It was something that didn't happen. For my hometown of Black Mountain, North Carolina, that was unique. They still talk about it 20 years later. He is an unbelievable speaker, and he is unbelievable with the parents. He made my parents feel comfortable. I can't say that about every coach that came in, so that was a big selling point. I just remember his connection with people.

He got into their world. He got into my mom's world—she's an assistant principal. He got into my dad's world—he ran summer camps. I'm sure Coach was briefed on me pretty good. He knew about our family. He was genuine, and that took him a long way.

Florida State didn't really recruit a lot of guys outside of the state of Florida at that time. Tallahassee's a long way away from home, but at the time, I thought the Florida State program was on the rise. Coach Bobby Bowden had the program going. I felt the school was first class. Everything about the program was first class. I asked myself, how are we going to travel? How do they treat their players? I just thought everything was set up there for us. What stands out the most about Coach Bowden is that he did it the right way for his players.

I liked the coaches. When you think about it, there are nightmares across the country with coaches. One coach is going to the pros. Another coach is being fired. At Florida State, there was stability. The question when I came here was, would Coach Bowden go to the pros or go to Alabama? I asked him, and he said, "No, I'm happy at Florida State." So I felt really comfortable in making a home there. I kind of made a decision to live there 20 years ago.

AT THE END OF THE DAY

Coming in as a freshman quarterback, I heard them say that I was not going to play until I was a junior. Casey Weldon and I were the first quarterbacks since Wally Woodham and Jimmy Jordan, who were in the same junior class. That was what was different about the whole situation. Chip Ferguson and PT Willis had been in the same year, but the coaches had separated them through redshirting.

At that time, it was always understood you would wait your time and then you would get two years as the starter. Coach Bowden made a switch after I started six games as a junior. I didn't think what happened to me was deserved or was handled well, but I never went in there and complained about playing time, which is very common. Coach Bowden did, however, say his door was always open if I needed to talk to him. It wasn't a fearful thing to see him.

There might be places where it might be fearful to approach the coach. Not there.

I talked to him twice about my own situation. Once was to go play basketball, and the other was after I got benched. That time he told me, "Keep working. Get better. You never know when you'll get another chance." And I was like, "Yeah, I hope for another chance." Coach Bowden and I had that conversation when it was over. What happened first was a meeting with quarterbacks coach Mark Richt, who said the team just needed a spark and something different. Casey brought a little flair to them, and it ended up being a good decision.

Even as a junior, after it happened, I still thought I was a late bloomer. I could hang my hat a little bit on the thought that I would eventually get some playing time. I was just hoping for another opportunity. I only got one game after that to really play, and that was against Louisville my senior year. The hard part for me was that Casey was being promoted for the Heisman Trophy, which was the first time that was done at Florida State.

At the time, I had the thought of transferring as a junior. I would get just one more year if I went to another school. I thought the best bet at the end of the day was to stay because of my original goal of being seen at Florida State by scouts.

FOOTBALL VERSUS BASKETBALL

When I got to Florida State, my whole thing was that I wanted to play basketball. That was my love completely. I didn't miss a day of basketball from the fourth grade to my sophomore year in college except on game days. So even on Sunday, I was playing basketball somewhere. My goal was to play Division I basketball. I didn't like football as much until I got a chance to actually play my junior year at Florida State. I didn't really start getting good at football until my third year in the pros, when I finally got comfortable with the game.

I did not have a full understanding that I could play both sports when I came here. The coaches kind of said, "If you want to play two sports, you can."

Brad Johnson went from FSU backup to Super Bowl–winning quarterback and credits much of his NFL success to what he learned under Bowden at FSU.
Courtesy of FSU Sports Information/Russ Obley

Where playing basketball caught up with me was spring football. The first spring in 1988 was OK because Casey and I were not getting any reps in practice, so that was not a big deal. But it caught up with me the next year. I missed 10 days of spring football in 1989 because the basketball team was in the NCAA tournament. That's when Coach Bowden said, "You're never going to make it. You have to decide how badly you really want to play football. You can play basketball—it's your thing. But in football, you're judged on 20 days of spring practice."

HE HAS A KNACK

When I signed and got to FSU, Coach Bowden would spend more time with the quarterbacks. His whole thing was throwing the "9 route"—the take-offs. We had great, physical, tall athletes at receiver. When he explained how to throw the 9 route, he said his goal was to at least give the receivers a chance to catch it—not to throw it flat. He would talk about the flight of the ball, and on the blackboard he would draw a mountain and the quarterback shooting an arrow over it. He drew the actual bow and arrow, and he drew an offensive receiver and a defensive player, and they were stick figures.

We tried not to laugh. We didn't know if he was joking or not, but he was dead serious. Coach Bowden was a quarterback in college. I never saw him throw the football, but I don't think he threw a good ball. He never did throw the football to demonstrate, but to me, that's the greatness of a teacher.

What he got into was the play fake. The play might be R44, and the play fake off of that would be R344 Cadillac. He would come over to us when we practiced it, and he would try to decide who had the ball. He would make it a guessing game—either the quarterback had it or the running back had it. So one time that we did it, we had two footballs, and he didn't know it.

He was into special plays, and he had a knack for calling them. I remember he was calling the plays in spring football, and the play was RC268 Cobra. There was a corner route by the slot receiver and a hitch by the split end on the same side. He called it the first time, and he called it again for the next play. I thought that maybe he had forgotten he called the same play twice in a row. He just said, "I think we can hit it again," and we did hit the corner route the next time.

He really just had a knack. If he saw something in a play, he would put a little extra emphasis on that play—like the Chris Weinke play against Clemson in 2000 where he tucked the ball and he turned his back deep in the end zone and then threw it for a 98-yard touchdown. He would look for those particular plays, and he would hold a special meeting for each play, and we would make it work.

He wouldn't watch film with us, but when he came in with an idea, you knew he had done his research on it. He might have had ideas for only five plays or 10 plays, but those five or 10 would be called.

The all-time greatest play fake, of course, was the Puntrooskie—the fake punt against Clemson in 1988. I was watching it in the game, and I thought the ball had been accidentally snapped over the punter's head too. The knack Coach Bowden had for calling the play at the right time—a reverse on our 10-yard line, something that you shouldn't do—that's why a coach has a long career or why he doesn't.

But mostly the offense was as basic as you could get it back in the day. The shotgun wasn't put in until later with Charlie Ward. There wasn't even a three-wide set before Charlie and offensive coordinator Mark Richt kind of took over. That's where football kind of was back then.

THE COMPONENTS OF GREATNESS

Coach Bowden would always have two backs, and that's another great thing about him. He kept Sammie Smith, Dexter Carter, Edgar Bennett, Amp Lee, Chris Parker, Keith Ross, Dayne Williams, and Marion Butts all happy. The greatness was how everybody played for each other and put their egos aside. Somehow, Coach Bowden kept everybody happy, and everyone put out for the one common goal, to win.

You found that same unselfishness with the quarterbacks. You looked at that quarterbacks meeting room, in that little cubicle, there were so many of us. When Coach Daryl Dickey was there the first time in 1989 as our coach, it was Peter Tom Willis, Casey, me, Charlie Ward, and Kenny Felder. That's pretty unique, and they kept us happy. Coach Bowden kept everybody focused on the goal so that there wasn't a hate thing between players. Take the quarterbacks—we were friends.

We thought Coach Bowden was a legend then—winning 200 games. We thought that was the pinnacle. We didn't know what it would grow into. It was an honor to play for him, and we did not want to let him down, that's for sure.

The program didn't bring in bad people. Maybe some bad things have occurred, but I think we were all good people.

Coach Bowden let his players grow. If you wanted to say something to the media, it was open. If we didn't want to say something nice or were going to be negative, we didn't say it. We said, "No comment." But Coach pushed us each to be our own person. He let us have the freedom. Sometimes that could bite us. He would say, "You're going to live with the consequences," but he never held us back for something we would say.

I thought he had unbelievable vision in selecting players. That's where you win it, in recruiting. And he had talented players. He knows his football, and he knows his players, and knows what his players can do.

I think another greatness of Coach Bowden is that he surrounds himself with great people—coaches, trainers, and the PR people who have been here forever too. There is great stability. If you are not hiring and firing, that means you probably did pretty good.

He had vision in selecting his coaches too. To take Mark Richt on as a graduate assistant at 24 and let him have the quarterbacks—there's something about that. He had been in the Miami program, and Coach Bowden knew he was smart and had a vision for him. He had the vision to hire Brad Scott as his coordinator after Wayne McDuffie and then to hire Mark as the coordinator after that.

I think he had a vision for the program. The goal was to win national championships. He also wanted to build a tradition where guys would come back. In the off-season, they let former players in the strength room. If we need the trainers, they let us use the trainers. He's even asked me to come out and throw with the guys at times. That says something to the next guy: "That's how you are going to be treated when you leave. They accept us back."

Another thing that really stood out about Coach was that he was very fierce in his competitiveness. You could never intimidate him. He wanted it bad. That's why he demanded the competition in practice and in mat drills. What you did in February and March and April would carry over to the next season and into life. He wanted to win, but he was not throwing chairs. He was very fierce and competitive—you could just feel it.

Even when I'm playing golf with him now—I can tell—it's in him. He hits the ball right down the middle. It is competitive to him. He doesn't like to lose.

WILLIAM FLOYD

---◄═☀═►---

THE CONSTANT VISITOR

One of the first things that Bobby Bowden tells parents and Florida State prospects during the recruiting process is that he has an open-door policy. If a Florida State football player has something on his mind or just wants to visit, Bowden encourages that player to come knocking on the door of his office that now overlooks the football field at Doak Campbell Stadium. Sometimes Bowden prompts the visits if he believes an issue needs to be addressed.

No Seminole player is believed to have visited with Bowden in his office more than William Floyd. They talked about everything—from Floyd's concerns about playing time in his first season in 1990 to Floyd becoming a father while still at FSU. The connection continued during Floyd's playing days as a starting fullback on the 1993 national championship team and through the running back's NFL career and beyond.

Floyd, a first-round pick of the San Francisco 49ers in 1994, earned a Super Bowl ring with that team the next season. He also played with the Carolina Panthers and retired after the 2001 NFL season. When his football career ended, Floyd became a businessman in Central Florida. But he continues to make time to travel with FSU during the football season, and in the spring of 2006, he accompanied Bowden on a number of stops during the annual Seminole Boosters tour throughout Florida.

Floyd is finishing the undergraduate degree that was put on hold while he played in the NFL. The plan is to earn the degree in the spring of 2007. The first invitation to commencement will be sent to Bobby Bowden.

It all started my first year at Florida State. I was redshirted and could not play that season. I went to see Coach Bowden about why I wasn't playing and why I would be redshirted. I felt like I could compete with the guys that were ahead of me, so I went into his office and sat down, and we talked about my situation. When I went into his office, I was kind of in awe. It seemed his chair was higher than all the other chairs in the room. There was all that stuff from his coaching career and life on the wall and the shelves. The visits evolved from me worrying about my playing time and talking about my redshirt to us focusing more on just everyday life. He always said his door was open and if there was anything going on, not to hesitate to come by and visit. He said that to all the players. I don't know how many did that. But to me that was the open invitation. And I used that fully. I would go up there at least once a week and maybe a couple of times. It got to the point where Miss Sue, Coach Bowden's secretary, would just wave me on in into his office.

I was a young father. My oldest son was born when I was in my second year of college—in '91, when I was just 19. I never will forget going in and talking to Coach Bowden about it. I told him that I had a kid on the way. I asked him if he thought it would be a good idea to get married. Of course, he is from that old school that if you have a kid on the way, you should do the right thing and get married. I wasn't ready for that at the time, but it still ended up working out his way because I ended up marrying my son's mom.

Coach would also talk about the responsibilities that I had as a father. He would ask me what was going on. He wanted any player who was a father to do the right thing with his kid.

He can be really serious, but he can be a funny guy, too. We didn't talk about politics or anything like that. We talked some about faith. We would pray as a team before a game, and he would tell us, "If you don't believe in the same God I believe in, that's no problem. While we're saying the Lord's Prayer, you pray to whatever God you pray to." Coach Bowden didn't stick religion in your face. He let you know he was a Christian, but he wasn't going to beat you over the head with it.

That's the way it was when we met. It wasn't always about football and Xs and Os. We didn't talk much Xs and Os except that I would talk to him about getting more carries with the ball. Later in my career, he would tell me I didn't have to worry about carrying the ball, and I trusted what he said. He would say, "Just take care of your business, and if you do, you'll go in the first or second round in the NFL."

A college kid's life is more about his family at home, missing home, and in my case, having a small child. That's what we talked about. I did learn a lot from him talking about his background. When I went in to see Coach Bowden, I was in there to talk to him like he was my father. I can't say that he gave me just one great piece of advice that I've always followed. There was a lot that I took from my talks with Coach Bowden, a lot of it with life lessons from what he had seen and experienced.

All those times we talked during my career, I always found him old-fashioned on core values. That was never going to change with him. I'm pretty sure the way he was on that was the way he was when he was young. It was the way he was brought up and also had to do with his faith. But as far as changing with the times, Coach Bowden has always been able to adapt and relate to his players.

THE MISCHIEVOUS SON

Coach Bowden would call me his mischievous son. I wasn't bad, but I was just always into something. I will never forget the first time he had to discipline me. That was the year I was redshirting and was unable to play in games. I wasn't having the best time in Tallahassee. I'd get bored. We were playing around in the locker room after practice, and I threw a tub of foot powder on somebody in the shower. Coach Bowden found out about it.

If you are redshirting, you get to pick one game that you can travel with the team. And that year, in '90, the game I picked was Miami in Miami. It was being played in early October, and I had been waiting for that game. Of course, it's always big and was going to be my first opportunity to really experience something like that on the road. I ended up not being able to go on that trip because I threw that tub of foot powder on somebody in the shower. That was Coach

William Floyd owns a Super Bowl ring and a national championship ring, but when he adds another prized possession in 2007—a diploma—Bobby Bowden will be the first he invites to the graduation ceremony.
Courtesy of Ryals Lee, FSU Photo Lab

Bowden's decision. To somebody on the outside, it may not look like much, but it really hurt me not to go on that trip.

You did not want Coach Bowden to be the one handing out the discipline. His discipline is a lot harder than anybody else's discipline. As players, we would deal a lot with his assistants, but we knew it was Coach Bowden's program. We all understood that.

Years after I left, Coach Bowden said that Florida State football is not a democracy. It's a dictatorship. It was kind of funny when he said every coach has a vote. They had eight votes. He had nine. There would be things that we could talk to him about. He might make some changes over time or do something subtly over time. But it was going to be his way.

There was another time at the end of that redshirt year I was trying to get a fake driver's license. I ended up getting in trouble for it, and the police came by. I went to see Coach Bowden, and he looked me in the eye and said, "William, I probably should send you home. But you're not bad; you're mischievous." If I had been a football player anywhere else, I would probably have been sent home for trying to get that fake driver's license. But Coach Bowden saw enough in me and saw what kind of person I was. He gave me a chance to prove him right.

From that point on, I really wanted to do right for him. He would not give up on a guy. He would go to the wire for you. There were guys who got into some things when I was at Florida State, but Coach Bowden always had your back as long as you did him right. He had expectations for each one of his players. You couldn't lie to him. And that's something that those who played for him still talk about and really appreciated about him.

For a lot of the guys, it was important to have somebody like him, somebody who believed in you, on your side. We had players who would do anything for him and work hard for him. Those of us who came to Florida State in '89, '90, and '91 took it upon ourselves to make our goal to win the first national championship for Coach Bowden. We wanted it for ourselves, but we really wanted to win it for Coach Bowden. We wanted to play for Coach Bowden, and we wanted to win for him. And he had a way to make us play for him. I think a lot of that also had to do with the trust he put in his players.

At the beginning of every football game, he would say to me, "Hey William, we're going to run the 45 Power, and we want you to set the tone." That was done almost every game my last year in school, and that was the '93 season where we won that national championship for him. For Coach Bowden to tell me that in front of the whole team— that on the first play of the game we were going to run that 45 Power, which means the fullback gets the lead block on the linebacker—was a challenge to me. I think he would challenge guys who he knew would take it in a positive way—that it would be a matter of pride, and they would get the job done. He knew the personalities of his players and which buttons to push with each one. That's why I think he will go down as the greatest coach of all time—the way he could get the most out of his players. Coach Bowden, in my opinion, was a fair man. And I think that had a lot to do with the way the guys played for him.

CHAMPIONS AT LAST

By the time I was at Florida State and playing, we were winning most of our games. But when we did lose, like to Notre Dame in '93, the coaches would challenge us by saying that somebody would have to pay for that loss. We had just two games remaining in the regular season after we lost to Notre Dame, and it was our only loss. I remember up in Thomasville, Georgia, the next week and the Friday night before we played NC State at home, the thinking was that we had probably messed up our chance for the national championship. But we were going to go out there and play hard just in case. That was Coach Bowden's approach. He always found a positive.

It just so happened that as we came back from Thomasville to Tallahassee to play NC State, the Notre Dame–Boston College game was on the radio on the bus. We were getting calls that Boston College was about to win. We were back in Burt Reynolds Hall when Boston College kicked that field goal to win the game. That was the craziest thing I had ever seen. Everybody was coming out of their rooms screaming. And then we won our game against NC State, and we were right back in it for the national championship. That goes back to

Coach Bowden that week. He had prepared us to beat NC State. He didn't give up on us, and we went out there and put a good thumping on NC State. We won 62–3.

Coach Bowden and the staff worked us hard. The mat drills, our practices—everything. We understood it was for one purpose, and that was to win a national championship. That's all we had to play for—there was no conference and no Bowl Championship Series bowls. It was the national championship. To achieve that goal, Coach Bowden's way was to have us better conditioned than anybody else.

Winning the national championship and winning it for Coach Bowden was a great experience. It was great to get that championship and to see the excitement around him and the look he had after the game. It is something I will always remember. For me, the other great thing was also having a father-son relationship with Coach Bowden. I didn't have a father in the house growing up, and one of the things Coach Bowden told my mom was that he would treat me like a son. I love him, and it's something that I tell him all the time. I couldn't have been the player I was or the man I was without having known Coach Bowden.

I believe all the guys who came to Florida State had an opportunity to have that kind of relationship. He meant it when he said that door was open. Some guys took advantage of that more than others, and I was one of those guys. And I'm glad I was, because I grew a lot from that experience.

DERRICK BROOKS

THE ALL-PRO

Bobby Bowden has said that he had a sense about Derrick Brooks from the moment they first talked at length during a home visit while recruiting the Pensacola native. The 1990 USA Today *High School Defensive Player of the Year and high school honor student with a 3.94 grade point average had the makings of something special at Florida State both on and off the football field. Bowden didn't know just how special.*

Brooks arrived in Tallahassee as a safety in 1991 and became a two-time All-America linebacker known for making the big plays. During FSU's 1993 national championship season, Brooks' junior year, he scored three touchdowns on fumble returns and had two interceptions. That effort also helped Brooks become the ACC Defensive Player of the Year.

His only off-field blemish occurred that season when he was found in violation of the NCAA's extra-benefit rule. Although Brooks was not part of the agent-financed Foot Locker shopping spree in November 1993, which became a national story as the first chronicled association with agents and a high-profile team, the violation cost Brooks the first two games of the 1994 season as part of the school's self-imposed rules. Brooks wasted no time in putting together a strong finish to his senior season. He forced a fumble, blocked a punt, made a sack, and snared an interception against Wake Forest in his first game back. By season's end, he added a postgraduate scholarship from the National Football Foundation and CoSIDA All-America honors to the honors he earned on the football field.

The accolades didn't stop for Brooks, who attained his master's degree from FSU after returning in the off-seasons. The 1995 first-round draft pick of the Tampa Bay Buccaneers earned All-Pro honors under coach Tony Dungy and led Tampa Bay to its first Super Bowl title in January 2003 with coach Jon Gruden.

Later Brooks admitted that his first title with FSU was even more memorable. "It was a feeling like no other," he said. "I think about that team all the time."

In addition to All-Pro honors with the Bucs, he was named 2000 NFL Man of the Year for his work with youth. He also received the Bart Starr award in 2003. He has treated members of the Boys and Girls Clubs to trips to places such as South Africa and Washington D.C.

In 2003, he was appointed by Governor Jeb Bush to the Florida State University Board of Trustees, the school's governing board.

The first time I met Coach Bowden was on an unofficial visit to Florida State. I wasn't a high priority at that time, and it was very short. "Hi. Bye." The next time I met Coach was on his recruiting visit in 1991 to my house in Pensacola. That home visit was much different.

It was me, my mom and dad, my little brother, and my little sister, Latoya—she was about four or five years old at the time. Coach Mickey Andrews was also there with Coach Bowden. Florida State, Miami, Notre Dame, and Auburn were among the schools recruiting me. We were all talking when my sister came into the room and went to sit next to me. I was sitting next to Coach Bowden, and Coach Andrews was standing up and talking.

Coach Bowden grabbed my sister and said, "Come sit in my lap, young lady."

So Latoya sat in his lap. During the course of about an hour or so of us talking, she kind of leaned over and fell asleep in his lap. It was funny because my mom went to grab her to put her in bed, and Coach Bowden said, "Nah, nah, don't disturb her. Let her sit right here."

That kind of sealed the deal for me—that and fact my best friend, Raymond Donald, had committed to FSU's basketball program. I was going to Florida State.

That's one of those abilities that just makes him who he is—he does a good job of relating to people in such a short period of time. As a head coach, you have to be able to make adjustments to different kinds of people and to different generations, and that's something he does very well.

When he's recruiting, he really gets to know the family and the players. And he and the assistants have done a good job of keeping it real. I was the top defensive player in the country in high school, but he didn't promise me anything but an opportunity to compete, play for a national championship, and get a degree.

My parents didn't really ask much about football during Coach's home visit. They wanted to know, "How are you going to take care of our son's needs? Are you going to make sure he goes to class and gets his degree?"

Football was something in my household that was secondary. My family was more concerned about how this was all going to correlate with me getting a degree. I was the first generation to attend college, and I think that's why they were so concerned that the student part of *student-athlete* be emphasized.

Coach Bowden has always challenged me to do my best academically. My freshman year, I didn't get the freshman academic award. I lost it to Aaron Dely by a couple points, and Coach called me in. He said that he expected me to win the academic award for best in the 1991 class. That catches your attention right there. I'll always remember him saying, "I expect you to have the highest GPA of your class every year. This is an award I think you should win every year."

It was always clear to me that those kind of accomplishments were important to him and made him proud.

AN ICON MOMENT

Of course, the highlight of my time at FSU was winning the national championship in 1993. I really didn't appreciate and understand the moment until we got back to the team hotel after beating Nebraska in the Orange Bowl. I was on the field doing television interviews and came in late for Coach's talk to the team. I only was around just a little bit in the locker room.

But at the hotel, that's when you saw the madness and joy of what we had just accomplished. There were so many ex-players who had been just one or two plays short of winning a national championship themselves, and to see how excited they were made you understand the moment. It felt like they had been on the field and had played the game, too. There were all those teams that were so close, and were so good, and we finally did it. That's when it kind of hit me that we had just accomplished this tremendous feat of bringing a national championship to Florida State and, in particular, to Bobby Bowden.

In the hotel and the next day on the plane, I sat back and watched. And that's the first time I really saw how important Coach Bowden was to college football. People say you look for an icon moment; I think that was really it when I saw him at the hotel and everybody was so congratulatory toward him and so happy for him. That was definitely my we-have-an-icon-as-a-coach kind of moment. You really saw the importance of him to so many people, and the importance of winning the national championship to the program.

From the beginning, I think that season said a lot about Coach Bowden and his staff. Our mentality was that of domination. For our defense in '93, everything was so personal. I clearly remember us working out that summer and already having an attitude that refused to let the team fail. We were going to be different. We were going to win a national championship on defense. With Florida State, there was always a lot of talk about the offense, about Charlie Ward; but Coach Bowden always talked about winning championships with defense.

We worked to dominate everything we did—from every drill we did that summer when the coaches weren't around to the weight room to the players going on the fields in the afternoon. I remember this workout we did on our own with area players in the summer. We went out and destroyed those guys. The defense, we didn't give up a yard. It's that kind of stuff you didn't hear about that defense and that team.

You could see the kind of season we were going to have just building up. In the goal-line drills in two-a-days, we didn't let the offense score a lick. Our goal was always to find one more play in ourselves.

It was more from the players. We had great players. And with every great player you need role players, and we had that. We had great

All-Pro linebacker Derrick Brooks (R) keeps tabs on Florida State football as a Board of Trustees member and plays for Tampa Bay in the NFL.
Courtesy of FSU Sports Information

chemistry, and you have to have that. We really did have guys who understood their roles and played to the best of their ability. They understood that when the ball was snapped, "This is my role, and if I don't play my role, then we will not be successful."

There has to be a group of players who give it everything they have, and that has to begin in the off-season. Coach Bowden didn't have to say, "Guys, we need you working hard. I need you working late."

The chemistry that Coach Bowden always talks about—*that* must come from within. It was there on that team. Everybody believed in the same goal at the time, and that goal was simply that we were going to dominate college football.

It wasn't about who was going to the NFL. It wasn't about who could chase the most women. We were going to do everything right because we wanted to be dominating. If things didn't go right, we dealt with it. The coaches didn't have to.

Coach Bowden left the defense more to Mickey Andrews during the week. But during the ball games, and in his Friday night speeches, he would say, "I don't expect anybody to score on the defense. Defense, I expect you to score."

I remember at North Carolina that season, we were ahead just 10–7 at halftime when he said, "Defense, it's time to stop playing around with these guys. Put them away."

That's all he said.

At Notre Dame, we were down 21–7 at halftime. Coach Bowden said, "Offense, keep doing what you are doing. Defense will get us back in the game."

It meant a lot for Coach to say that, but at the same time, it was what we expected to do, too. Having the head coach get up there and say what he did was going to stir some emotions. He expected us to dominate every single snap. That mentality prepared us for the NFL, and some of the best competition I had was in practice. The guys I was going against made the games easier in a sense, and at the same time, those practices prepared us for the NFL. The conditioning program we went through—I would have a hard time going back and making that conditioning test right now. I would need three or four months to train for that.

FOOT LOCKER AND THE NCAA

In my opinion, Coach Bowden was angry at the process because we had not violated any particular NCAA rule. The NCAA dug up this extra-benefit rule. To me personally, it felt like the NCAA was taking his football team and the discipline of his football team out of his hands, meaning he had a certain way that he was going to discipline us for—in his terms—"making a bad decision." Anytime anybody gets in the way of him doing that, he gets very upset. I think he was very unhappy that he had come up with a plan on how he was going to discipline us, but the NCAA had undermined his plan to discipline.

Coach Bowden realized we were in the wrong place at the wrong time and that we made a bad decision. And he was going to reprimand us. The reprimands we received—were they harsh enough? Who knows? But he suspended us for the summer, so we had to go back home and couldn't work out with the team. He didn't allow us to be part of the team, and believe me, that hurt us a lot. So he had already started the process of reprimanding us.

And I think he looked at how other schools were being treated that were in the same situation. He saw how the NCAA was handling them and how they were handling us, and he felt we were being targeted. And I still believe to this day that we were. At that time, the NCAA was looking to pin something on Florida State, and they hadn't been able to. That's why they went and researched the extra-benefits rule. They dusted that off. We didn't violate agent rules, but it was the extra-benefits rule that could involve an ordinary citizen giving us something. They were definitely looking to get us, and they accomplished that to a certain extent.

A CHANGING RELATIONSHIP

Prior to joining the FSU Board of Trustees, I would talk with Coach Bowden at least twice a year. Because I play for Tampa Bay, he is able to follow my career more closely than others. And I know he watches NFL games when he can to see the Florida State guys who are playing. He tells me how proud he is of his players playing in the NFL, and he always makes sure to talk about us saving our money so we can have something to fall back on whenever our football careers end.

I talk to Coach Bowden more now because of my Board of Trustees position. My relationship with him has changed, but that is the nature of what we have to do. For me to be successful in that role, it has had to change.

I'm trying to find out what that defining moment for the current FSU program is going to be. Do they go back and find what we had— what I like to think of as a national championship–type of attitude? It is going to happen. There will be a group of players who reach deep down and find it.

We had coaches who told us what we needed to hear, not what we wanted to hear. It's hard to make changes and deal with changes. Coach

Bowden didn't have to worry about losing assistant coaches for 14, 15 years. And then he had *that* happen—coaches going to other places and getting better offers. It has been an adjustment period for him.

He's a positive person. Period. And that's the first thing he tries to interject into a situation—whether we are behind in a game or after we lose a game or anything else. He tries to look on the bright side. When you are in the business he is in, and dealing with as many people as he is, you want to get across a positive vibe. A lot of people are going to react to what they see in him. If he's negative, then that will be their response. I have always seen him trying to stay positive, no matter the situation. But that positiveness, it can blind you, too.

BLESSED

To me, Coach Bowden is a man of God—a persistent, loyal person and the best of all time in college football. I'm not just talking wins.

In my opinion, Coach Bowden should be remembered as the very best college football coach. Personally, I'll remember him as a man of God who is faith-driven. I took his Friday night testimonies before games to heart.

He should be remembered for his persistence, because not everybody can do what he has done for so long. I don't think it's easy. And there is a consistency in who he is. What you see is what you are going to get. That hasn't changed one bit.

Coach Bowden is a caring person. He'll ask about your family, now maybe more with me than he did when I was in school. When you are in school, a lot of that is done by the coach who recruited you. For me, that was Mickey Andrews.

I've been really blessed to have been around Coach Bowden and Coach Dungy. Those two icons in my life have shaped me in a way that still influences me today. They uphold the high standards. In this business, for them to emphasize the other things outside of football—the important things—first, I can't put it any way but to say I am blessed.

JIM GLADDEN

⊰••⊱—⊰○⊱—⊰••⊱

THE LOYAL ASSISTANT

The continuity of Bobby Bowden's staff has been the envy of college football coaches nationwide. Ten coaches spent at least a dozen seasons with Bowden as a full-time coach, and three were with Bowden for more than 20 years.

Of the original staff Bowden hired in 1976, no coach stayed longer than Jim Gladden, who in 2001 retired after 26 seasons under Bowden. The defensive assistant coach counted Lombardi Award winners Jamal Reynolds and Andre Wadsworth and All-Americans Peter Boulware and Reinard Wilson among his pupils.

Gladden had been a graduate assistant under Darrell Mudra until Mudra was fired, and he then oversaw some of the administrative and recruiting responsibilities during the transition. Gladden wasn't even sure he would be hired when Bowden arrived in Tallahassee to rebuild the FSU football program.

Gladden spent those days doing everything from cleaning blackboards to running errands as Bowden's gopher. Bowden rewarded the loyalty, and Gladden returned it to him for more than 25 years.

In our first staff meeting in 1976, Coach Bowden sat us all down and laid out his goals. He had long-range goals and short-range goals.

The long-range goals were for us to be a contender for a championship of some sort and to be in the bowl picture every year. Because we weren't in a conference, that had to be the major goal—to be in a bowl.

The short-range goal was to play for respectability, to try to build the program to a respected position. He let it be known that there were three things he wanted from his players. (1) Character. (2) Guys that would fight and not quit. "Let's bring in fighters," he would say. "I've seen too many good players and athletes who were great players but who did not want to fight." (3) Guys who wanted an education. There was a history of poor judgment over who we brought in from other programs; we brought in some guys who had flunked out. Coach Bowden said that we would win the games that we had a chance to win with the kind of guys who exhibited those three qualities.

Coach Bowden wanted an athlete who was good enough that he could be a player and not a political appointee or just a guy hanging on. Coach Bowden wanted us to beat Florida, but he knew it was unreasonable for us to think we could go head to head and get five out of five recruits. If we got one out of five or two out of five, that would be good.

In that meeting, Coach Bowden expressed his expectations for his coaches, saying he wanted to surround himself with guys who had family values. At that time, he wouldn't hire you if you were divorced. He didn't want that. He said, "If you get a divorce, you better look for a job." He said, "I don't want a womanizer. And I don't want to hear about a guy out around town drinking."

He took the administrative responsibilities and divided them up like pieces of a pie. Each coach had a responsibility. He was the first person I knew of in the business who ever laid down those expectations on paper. He would hand a paper to me that read, "Jim Gladden. Coaching responsibilities—coach the defensive ends and outside linebackers. Recruiting responsibilities—recruit South Georgia, North Florida, and all of Texas that you can get to. Other duties—dorm director or liaison between the cafeteria and the coaching staff; head up the spring coaching clinic or run the camp."

Probably the best thing about Coach Bowden was his management skill. When he handed me that sheet with my responsibilities, he would say, "Jim, this is what your job is. I want you to become the expert at your position—the best and most knowledgeable guy you can be. If that means going out and visiting pro camps and other coaches who have been successful at your position, you do that."

In his 26 seasons on Bobby Bowden's staff, Jim Gladden came to appreciate his managerial style. *Courtesy of FSU Sports Information*

He would say, "I don't want a yes-man. I want a guy who will argue with me and try to make a point. I want input." Then he would say, "I'm not going to tell you how to do your job. If you can't do it, there is no need for me to have you on this staff. You put your own spin on it. I'm not going to look over your shoulders. It's your job."

I was the associate head coach in my last couple of years, after Chuck Amato left following the 1999 season. Coach told me, "I don't want to know all the problems. I've got you to handle the little stuff. If you can't handle the little stuff, and that gets up to me, I don't need you. You can handle all those dorm problems."

We had an incident that happened up at the dorm one time, and it got taken care of. I went to tell Coach about it, and his response was, "Why are you telling me? You handled it."

That kind of management style gave the coaches ownership in the program. It made us feel that the program was ours as much as it was his. He allowed us to be a strong part of the program. I think that's what carried us through all those years until we had a couple of guys leave in the 1990s. He didn't try to micromanage us. There was a special respect we all had for Coach, and it went back to how he handled us.

Coach never put rules like "no drinking" and "no womanizing" on paper. But he told them to us. And he did put down that the goal was to be the most accessible, friendliest staff in our state, in the Southeast, and in the country.

He would tell us, "If I ever hear of one of my coaches high-rolling a high school coach, you can find another job. I don't want to get a call from a coach saying, 'I haven't seen a Florida State coach come by here in two years.' I don't want that. It's your responsibility to go by and visit personally with that coach. When I call the roll in our hideaway meeting in the summer and go through that log with all the schools in this state and call out Winter Park High School, I don't want the guy recruiting that school to say, 'I went by.'" Coach Bowden said that he had a guy when he was up at West Virginia who would just drive by. He wanted us to visit those coaches and befriend those guys and win their respect. He said we were to do that by being available and by allowing them to ask questions. We were to spend as much time with a coach as he wanted to spend with us. That was Coach Bowden's philosophy.

Something else he would always say to the staff was "My security is your security. As long as I am secure, you're secure here."

GREAT TO COACH DEFENSE

Coach Bowden was very hands-on with the offense—always. He was always focused that way, always thinking, watching film, attending their meetings.

I'll never forget before the Florida game in 1977 when we were at the Holiday Inn in Ocala. The pregame meal was breakfast, and all the coaches were at the table. Coach had this napkin and was scripting the first eight or 10 plays. That was the 37–9 win in Gainesville, and those plays worked. We went right down and scored.

Another thing that was funny, and this was typical Bowden, in the Wednesday or Thursday morning staff meeting, he would ask offensive coordinator Mark Richt, "What's going to be our lead play on Saturday?"

Mark might answer, "46 Toss," and Coach would say, "Um, that's funny. How come we only ran that three times in practice with Warrick Dunn? How come he only got that three times? If that's your lead play, you ought to be running that 20 times."

You might think he wouldn't notice that up there in that tower on the practice field. But he sits up there, and he has a remarkable mind for seeing things and remembering them.

His intensity would not be the same with the defense unless we were facing an unbelievable challenge.

The first thing we did as a staff on Sunday when grading the game film was take the play-by-play and mark down what caused the breakdowns. That was because Coach would come in on Monday with his play-by-play and look at the film with us. Defensive coordinator Mickey Andrews might say the problem on a given play was a bad call—that we weren't in a good defense. And Coach Bowden was satisfied with that as long as we didn't try to pull the wool over his eyes. We weren't going to be able to do that.

It was great to coach the defense at Florida State because Coach left us alone for the most part. He would come up to us and say, "What are you going to do to stop them, buddy?" Or he would come down that sideline during a game and grab me by my sleeve and say, "Jim, can we get some pressure on that passer?" And I would answer, "Yeah, Coach, we're going to do it."

Then they would run the draw or throw a screen, and he would yell, "You better watch the screen."

But really, Coach's philosophy is if you try to defend everything, you end up defending nothing.

Then there was the Southern Mississippi game in 1981, where their quarterback, Reggie Collier, just ripped us apart, and we lost 58–14. Before we played at Southern Mississippi the next year, Coach Bowden came into our defensive meeting and said, "I don't care how you do it, but don't let that Collier guy beat us this year." He made certain we understood that. So we played the game to defend Collier. Their running back, Sam DeJarnette, went for more than 300 yards, but we did win the game.

After the 1980 season, we went through some years where we weren't very good on defense. The philosophy had become that we were going to take the best players and put them on offense. That started to change with Deion Sanders. Deion was an either-way guy as a receiver or cornerback. We told Deion that he would catch more passes over there at the corner in his freshman year than he would as a receiver. "Every time it goes up, you have a chance to get it," we told him. Coach Bowden backed us on that.

Coach is not a guy with a completely closed mind, but you have to prove to him that something else is better to get him to change. You have to come in there and be able to say, "If we do it this way, we can get more production," and show him how your way is better. For example, if you go in there and say, "Coach, So-and-so needs to be kicked off the team," you better have documentation. And that goes for plays too. You just don't come in and say, "32 Trap is not a good play." You have to show in detail how it is not working.

As a defensive staff, we decided that instead of sitting there in just a "read defense," maybe we could get more out of our personnel by looking at some different defenses. Miami's defensive line, for example, was attacking and creating problems for the offense. Mickey liked it, but he was afraid we didn't know enough about it. So we did what Coach Bowden had told us to do from the beginning: we went out and learned. I went down and spent a bunch of time with Miami coach Butch Davis.

Of course, Coach Bowden hired Mickey and was supportive of what we did—things like keeping Deion on defense. Deep down inside, Coach always believed you win with the kicking game and defense. He wasn't in our defensive meetings like he was with the offense, but we knew that defense was important to him.

The only instruction Coach Bowden had with us on defense was simply to play our best people. He would come down the line and say, "Do you have your best people out there, buddy? I get nervous when I see all those people running in and out. I look up and see four freshmen on the field. It scares me to death."

But our deal was to go to an attack scheme, and Mickey was very much the driving force on this—play as many people as you can. One, a tired guy can't play as well as a fresh guy. Two, by playing everyone, you're always working on next year's team. And three, morale is better, because everybody came to play.

Coach was skeptical and old school, but he was astute enough to see the results. He would question us on Monday. He never got on a coach in front of the team and never in a staff meeting. He would disagree with us in a staff meeting, but if he was mad and had a bone to pick with you, he'd call you in his office—just you and him. His goal was never to take a man's dignity away.

A couple of times he called me in and straightened me out on something. He would say, "Jim, you were wrong on that." Whether I believed I was right or not, I was wrong, and I knew it.

He had the ability to get on us without raising his voice and putting us on the defensive. He always approached us from a positive standpoint. Instead of saying, "You're dead wrong, and that's a bad job," it would be, "If we do it this way, I think we can get better."

You walked out of a talk with him thinking, "Coach is right on this. I've got to do better."

Bobby was not going to get on the headsets and get on a coach. He was going to get us on Monday, and probably in his office.

SUPERSTITIOUS YET RELIGIOUS

Coach Bowden was a very superstitious guy, extremely so. If you won in a certain uniform, he wanted the team to be in that uniform. If he wore a set of clothes, that is what he wanted to wear. He didn't want to change anything—not his shoes, not his belt. He was superstitious, but his faith was strong.

He gave testimonies on Friday night. First he began with talks based on matchups. Like when we played Florida and Emmitt Smith. We had Sammie Smith, and Coach would challenge our offensive line to get Sammie more yards than Emmitt did against our defense. "And Jamie Dukes, you are going against the All-America nose tackle at Nebraska. When the game is over, who will be the All-American?" That was his Friday night talk.

And when he was finished with that, he'd go through the Bible and take something and develop it into something that related to the team. Maybe there'd be a player who was not spiritual, and Coach's words might not take effect right then. But maybe 20 years down the road, that player will come back and say, "I remember that devotion, and this is how it helped me."

His faith really came out during the funeral for his grandson, Bowden, and his former son-in-law, John Madden. He said, "Don't feel sorry for them. They're not here. They're gone. I don't know why people come to funerals. If you come to mine, you're not going to see anything but a shell. Don't bother to come to mine, because I'm not going to be there. I know where I'm going to be."

IF HE FAILS, I FAIL

The first time we played Joe Paterno in the Blockbuster Bowl, Coach Bowden made it very, very clear to us that we had better find a way to win. Coach had never beaten Joe before, and we were not going to lose that game.

Losses eat at him. That 13–2 loss to Oklahoma in the national championship Orange Bowl after the 2000 season really upset him. We should have won the game. We were the better team—no doubt about it. Coach Bowden made the statement he would never go through that again, and that if ever he had a guy like Mark Richt who was going to take another job, as Richt did at Georgia in the days before that Orange Bowl, he would send him on his way.

The losses to Florida, next to a couple of championship opportunities that we missed in bowl games, probably hurt Coach Bowden the most. But Coach Bowden has always been able to keep them in perspective. There's no doubt he wants to win, but he does not want to win at all costs. He's not going to sell his soul to win. He's not going to sell his principles to win.

I've seen him compromise a little bit on his hard-line rules as far as dress and hair go. He's looked around and has seen other coaches that he respects who are allowing their players to wear their hair differently. But that's not a new approach for him. You can go back to Deion Sanders. Deion was different, but as long as he was not hurting somebody else or demeaning his opponent, then Coach didn't believe control over Deion's appearance was a battle he and his staff had to win. Coach has always been able to look out and see the big picture and say, "These are the battles we've got to win, and these are the ones I want to win."

You can look at Sebastian Janikowski or Mike Shumann when we first started here; there are guys who test Coach in just about every class of guys that has come along. His philosophy was made up when he was a senior at Howard College, where his football team was undefeated and was set to play Jacksonville State for the conference championship. The winner would go to the Tangerine Bowl. Coach Bowden told us that his Howard College coach came in and told the team the night before the game that three of their guys were not going to play because they were told not to go to a fair one night but went anyway. Coach Bowden said the team's heart just dropped because they knew they could not win the game without those guys.

He told us, "Right then and there, I made my mind up I would not sacrifice the team and its goals for one guy or two guys or three guys when I became a coach. I would not penalize my team for what one idiot did. There are all kinds of ways to penalize that guy without penalizing the other 90. You can run him at five o'clock in the morning or take him off the training table and let his parents pay for the food—that will sit real good with them—or take him off of scholarship."

That story was one he told us early on, and he told it again right after Sebastian Janikowski broke curfew before that 2000 Sugar Bowl. With Coach, discipline falls into two categories—misdemeanor or serious. With a misdemeanor—and this isn't just in terms of law but includes not showing up for class or workouts, or failing a drug test—you would get three strikes. He has always said, "Unless it's something like a felony, if we close the door on that guy, who out there is going to open one? If he fails, I fail."

If a player lies to him, then all bets are off. The same applies to coaches. You are as good as your word. If a coach tells one of his players that he will play on Saturday and then doesn't get that player into the game, that would really get under Coach Bowden's skin. He'd say, "Get him in there. You told him he would play. Don't tell him something and not do it."

NOT AN "I" GUY

What is good about working with Coach is that he is always good about giving his assistants credit. He's never put his chest out and said, "Look what I did." He's never been an "I" guy.

Although Coach Bowden is a private person, it's not like he is cold or distant. He's not like that. He's never met a stranger and made him feel comfortable. When he's talking to you, he looks at you. He's not looking over your shoulder to see if there is a more important person in the meeting across the room. But he does like his private time. When practice was over, he would go home. As a staff we did not do a lot of socializing outside of the command performances. And the command performances were things like recruiting dinners, the Christmas party at the Bowdens' house, the kickoff dinner before the season, and the annual fundraising cruise.

My years with Coach Bowden were wonderful. He always asked about my dad and mother. "Hey, buddy, have you called your mother this week? Well, you need to do that. We're not promised tomorrow." I appreciated that. There are some coaches whose minds that would never have crossed. They don't give a rip about your family. They couldn't care less.

TOMMY, TERRY, & JEFF BOWDEN

———•◦———○———◦•———

THE THREE COACHING SONS

Of Bobby Bowden's four sons, three went into coaching. Terry, while at Auburn, and Tommy at Tulane put together perfect seasons. Their father has accomplished that feat twice, once in 1999 with a staff that included son Jeff as the wide receivers coach.

———•◦———○———◦•———

TOMMY BOWDEN

Tommy Bowden played under his father at West Virginia and had two coaching stints under his dad at FSU. He learned a lot from his father, and parlayed that knowledge into victories over Bobby in 2003 and 2005.

And as his father did at FSU, Tommy Bowden has rebuilt programs. He inherited a Tulane program that went 4-7 in 1996 and two years later went 11-0 in the regular season. He took a Clemson program that went 3-8 before his arrival and coached them to 9-3 two years later. He begins his eighth season at Clemson in 2006.

I am not sure that there was anything in particular that made me want to be a coach. It was more of the overall environment during my youth. With my father's religious or Christian overtones, there was obviously some calling involved. But there wasn't one moment or one specific thing I saw in my dad as a coach that inspired me to enter his profession.

I was raised with a father that I respected simply because of his lifestyle, his relationship with his wife and family and the success of his marriage, and I admired the qualities I saw in him. He just happened to be a coach. And therefore, it became something I wanted to do.

I wrote an autobiography when I was in the sixth or seventh grade in which I said that I wanted to go into college coaching. I was either 12 or 13 years old, and from that point I was pretty much in one-track mode to be a coach. I knew early what I wanted to do. But it was much later when I started to watch my dad from the standpoint that I was going to be a coach and observed how he did it.

I was more interested in playing sports as opposed to building knowledge and preparing for my lifetime profession. I don't think I really started watching dad as a coach until I was a graduate assistant at Florida State in 1978. That's when I first started watching his play-calling, his preparation throughout the week and on Friday night, the discipline of his players, his management style during the games, and his handling of the media.

That is when I first started drawing from his coaching experience. Growing up, we didn't discuss football very much at all in the house. I can't remember conversations. He threw the football some with us, but he didn't play football with us. I can remember more of him hitting a baseball to us and throwing a baseball to us. I remember that more than I do Daddy playing football with us. We never went to sporting events with him. I never hunted with him. Daddy took us fishing once because he felt he had to.

But back to being a graduate assistant under him at Florida State—that was during the time in my coaching career when I was forming my philosophy. As a young coach, a lot of times the first impressions are the best impressions, and they are the most lasting impressions. At Florida State is where I began gathering those first impressions. I also played for him for four years at West Virginia. A lot of how he is as a motivator I first saw as a player. The talks at halftime and pregame, I experienced those first as a player. I was able to see how

In 1979, the only year all four were together at FSU, Jeff Bowden (88) was a backup receiver at FSU while older brother Tommy (L) and Terry (R) worked on their father's coaching staff. *Courtesy of FSU Sports Information*

he related with players firsthand, and I thought that was pretty beneficial to me later.

I can remember in 1974 at West Virginia, when he had that bad 4-7 season, a team meeting was called without the coaches. I was on the team and was at that meeting when players complained about doing too much hitting and practicing too long, and they complained about the play-calling. That was the only time as a player I remember hearing negative comments about how dad operated.

As a graduate assistant, I witnessed his staff management philosophy. He's always delegated responsibilities on defense, and he has been actively involved with the offense. I saw how he related with the staff and how he disciplined his players. I really think that when I went to Tulane in my first job as a head coach in 1997, I was well prepared because of experiences such as the one at Florida State. Looking back, I don't feel that I had to learn the job of head coach by trial and error.

Dad did things then as head coach that I didn't really appreciate the difficulty or challenge of until I became a head coach. Those three or four feet between one side of a head coach's desk and the other is a pretty big three or four feet. It's certainly not always easy to sit on the side he sits on and make the decisions he must make.

I was right in tune with Daddy's offensive philosophy until I went to Tulane, where I did not have the personnel he had. I really deviated at that particular time away from the Xs and Os I learned from him. I really had to do something unique and different to survive. I couldn't survive in the I-formation with a great tailback and dominant defense. I didn't have that available to me.

WHEN HE FALLS, HE DOESN'T FALL VERY FAR

From the point of being a head coach and looking at my dad's career, I think what impresses me the most is his level of consistency. His 14 consecutive 10-win seasons is an NCAA record. He finished each of those 14 seasons in the top five, and no other coach has done that.

When he falls, he doesn't fall very far. He falls to eight or nine wins, and that is not a fall in the real world of college football. Because of the standards he has set at Florida State, however, it may be perceived as a fall.

The consistency he has enjoyed certainly extends to many aspects of his program. Look at the consistency he has in maintaining staff. He hasn't had much turnover in his years at Florida State. He must be treating people fairly and honestly, or they wouldn't stay there. I contend that his staff management style is second to none, because coaches and other staff don't leave Florida State very often. The consistency in that area, or the staff longevity, has a lot to do with the fact that he delegates. He is not a micromanager. A staff likes to have some control and autonomy over their positions and what they do. And Dad allows that to happen.

In addition to the consistency, I think something else that is amazing is his ability to change with the times. He has been a head coach through six decades, and there have been a lot of social and cultural changes during that time. He has been able to adjust to those changes and the effect that they have on young people—his players. And Dad has been able to adjust to all the different players' personalities. I think that is an unusual quality. It's not easy to adjust like that.

As a coach, the best advice he gave me came when I was getting ready to go to East Carolina for my first full-time job when I was leaving Florida State after the 1979 season. He spoke to me about patience and perseverance. That always stuck with me in this profession.

From father to son, I would say the best advice is to have a godly foundation. If you take a godly foundation into your profession, you'll do things the right way in terms of how you treat players and treat coaches. The two are intertwined a little bit.

FATHER VERSUS SON

The challenge in preparing for playing against Dad and Florida State is that his teams are well coached. They are not going to give any freebies, and they have great players.

From having been in his locker room as a player and as a young coach, I know Daddy's halftime talks. I have a pretty good idea what is going to happen in the second half, because I have heard his talk. He's not a screamer. He doesn't holler. He just stays upbeat and points out that the team has to correct its mistakes. It's not so much that the Xs and Os are the most difficult part in playing him. It's the quality of the coaching on his staff, his ability to motivate, and the quality of their athletes.

Our family has talked a lot about how the games between us have changed since the first time we met as head coaches in 1999. I'm sure for the fans it is still a lot of fun. I think it is in our personality to hide from the pressure and the stress with humor. So there is a bit of that when we talk on the field before our games against each other. But mostly, we talk about how we played the week before, injuries, or how Jeff is doing. He'll ask about my kids, and I'll ask about Mother. It's just casual conversation. And that's really the way it is before a game with any coach I face except that I talk a little more personal with my dad.

During the game, the challenge comes because he is what I call "dumb like a fox." A lot of his success during his career has come from doing the unexpected. His opponents had better be prepared for that. He's not going to have a lot of tendencies.

Of course, we go up against each other in recruiting. The one most recently that stands out is the recruiting of running back C. J. Spiller, who we signed as part of our 2006 recruiting class. This particular prospect was a lifelong Florida State fan and Warrick Dunn fan, and he was from Florida. We knew that Florida State and Florida would be our biggest competition for him. It was difficult. My dad has always had a tremendously powerful influence over mothers and fathers, and he now appeals to the whole family—not only the middle-aged mother and father, but also their parents.

I've learned not to bring up his age and retirement. I stay away from that. Penn State coach Joe Paterno is going on 80, and Daddy is 76. I kid him about it, but I don't bring that up in the home of a prospect. It goes back to the story that is almost all true about my brother Terry and our first home visit together. He was the head coach at Auburn, and I was on his staff. We've embellished the story a little bit, but basically, Terry brought up that dad wouldn't be coaching much longer. Word of that got back to Daddy, and Daddy went around a week later and said, "I'll be at Florida State longer than he will be at Auburn." There was truth to that.

When I was an assistant coach at Alabama, we once recruited a prospect in Jacksonville who was also interested in Florida State. I called the prospect, and the mother answered. I said, "This is Coach Bowden," and I asked if so-and-so was in. I could hear the prospect in the background ask, "Which one is it? Is it the real one or the other one?" I was the other one.

A SON'S VIEW

What you see in Daddy is what you get. It really is that way. There's not any real deviation from that. It goes back to the consistency factor being such a big part of who he is.

I have not seen many changes in Dad other than the fact that as he has gotten older, he delegates more of the Xs and Os. He still stays active in staff management, motivation, and recruiting. I haven't seen changes in that except to adjust to the times and cultural changes. The changes are more in the game-day operations.

I think one of the difficulties of writing a book or doing a movie on Dad is that he didn't smuggle drugs or beat his wife or have several divorces or get in drunken stupors. His story would be pretty boring in that regard. He hasn't deviated too far from the golden path.

TERRY BOWDEN

As a kid who grew up loving sports, Terry Bowden quickly learned his calling wouldn't be as an athlete. He did play four seasons for West Virginia as a walk-on running back between 1975 and 1978, but his peers shot past him using their size and strength, so he gravitated into a more cerebral role. After heading to Florida State and earning his law degree, Terry Bowden opted to follow his father's career path into coaching.

At age 26, he landed the head coaching position at Salem College in West Virginia, becoming the youngest college football coach in the country. He took over a team that was winless the previous year. In two seasons, he led Salem to a conference title and a berth in the NAIA playoffs.

From there, he became head coach at Samford University, where his father was head coach when it was known as Howard College. That led to his career breakthrough, becoming head coach at Auburn, leading the team to an unbeaten season.

Now Terry Bowden is known for his voice. In addition to hosting a daily sports radio show in Orlando, he works for ABC Sports as a college football analyst, and he's also part of a motivational speaker circuit.

He resides in Orlando with wife, Shryl, and their children.

Looking back on my own coaching career, I think what enabled my early success in coaching is what I first learned from my father. I got my understanding of offensive football from him. I think that's what helped me to become the head coach at Salem College in West Virginia in 1983, back when I was 26 years old. I had been my father's self-scout coach at FSU as a volunteer assistant for three years.

I remembered every play Dad called. I charted every single play he called, and I did a self-scout. So every Friday night before a Florida State game, we'd go over the plan, and I would say, "Dad, this is what a particular opponent does on third-and-short, and this is what you do on third-and-short. This is what you do 83 percent of the time; this is what you never do." So by doing that, I knew every play he called on every down.

I called plays exactly like he did when I became head coach. After doing that for three years, I had all of that memorized. I ran a sprint draw on second-and-7. I ran this on fourth-and-short—stuff like that. Everything he did, I copied.

What's so interesting about my father is the plays he called, the offensive philosophy he maintained. It was the complete opposite of what his personal life was like from the standpoint that he took chances. He did unpredictable things offensively. It was the kind of stuff you would never see a lot of football coaches do.

But he would never do something unpredictable in his real life. He was very conservative. But as an offensive mind in football, it was the complete opposite, whether it would be the Puntrooskie play or the reverse near the goal line.

It is almost as if the game is a stage. And he knows he's in a game, not in real life. He's on the stage, and he can act a little bit. It's an alter ego, the stand-up comic role.

I always think of Dad as the stand-up comic who always knows how long to pause when he delivers the punch line and how to catch people off-guard. And to me, I will always see him in football terms as the stand-up comic who knows when to deliver a punch line in a game.

He knows when to set people up and build them up to the crescendo. His opponents think they know what to expect, but they get something else. His style of play-calling back then, back in the early '80s, was so different from the way a lot of coaches do it now.

I'm not sure how it would work now. The offense was much simpler. It was much less complicated than it is now. There might have only been five running plays and 15 different passing plays, but it was a case of knowing them so well he could call any play on first-and-10 and any play on fourth-and-inches.

And when a play was stopped, he'd know exactly why it got stopped and how to counter the one thing that stopped it. That was the philosophy he began with, and that's what I was taught. Once Florida State got the no-huddle, fast-break offense, it became a system where we never knew where the ball would be directed. I'm not sure it's been as effective.

I happen to think he could go back and win with that same stuff we did in '79 through '82. I know I won that way. I never changed much—only a little bit.

I got my start in coaching working for my father in 1979 as a volunteer assistant at Florida State. When I came to Tallahassee, my brother Tommy was a graduate assistant working with the secondary. I had also been accepted to law school at FSU, and I was taking 16 hours a semester.

Well, Dad wouldn't let me be a graduate assistant, because graduate assistants back then didn't have to go to class. He made me be a volunteer, so I got nothing. I got zero money and went to law school for 16 hours. I also got hired as a dorm manager. That's how I got my first divorce. I was a full-time student, working 16 hours, who would leave law school, go to the football coaches' offices in time for practice, get my cards ready, run the scout team, or whatever. I would then stay with my notebooks and work on my homework until 11 or 12, and then go out there and clean the pool out and do that stuff. That's how my days were spent, with no time in-between.

I was a volunteer every year for the three years I was at Florida State, going to law school. When I graduated from law school, I was a graduate assistant that following season.

What I learned from my father, what I took to heart and really tried to put into my own coaching style, was his overall offensive philosophy.

What I also took from Dad was that he was very thorough. He believed in having a plan for everything. I remember going up and copying everything in his files. He pretty much had a calendar from January 1 to December 31. He knew what to do every day. Everything was planned, so he made sure he was doing the right thing.

Dad's system was a good, solid system.

EARLY LIFE LESSONS

My father handled assistant coaches the same way he handled his children: he was firm but fair. He doesn't lose control that much—firm but fair. I think if you ask, players will say they were scared to go into his office and see him if they had done something wrong. It was almost as much about letting him down as it was a fear of him ripping into them.

In all my life, I think the worst I ever felt was the time I was a young teenager. Dad asked me to do something I didn't get done. And the next time he came home, he said, "Terry, I would rather you tell me you're not going to do something than to tell me you're going to do something and never do it."

That was with me all my life. That stuck with me more than anything.

I think firm and fair would fit his criteria more than anything else—not scary, not yelling.

It was the same way working for him. It wasn't like I was afraid of him, but I would just feel terrible. He was someone I did not want to displease. I wanted to get it done.

When I worked at Florida State, George Henshaw, who is now with the New Orleans Saints, was the offensive coordinator. Jack Stanton was defensive coordinator.

The meetings were relaxed. Dad was just like he is now. He's a fairly relaxed person. There was no fear. We didn't sit in a meeting worried that someone was going to be called out, because we knew he would never do that.

The meetings were never something that we hated to go into. There was a calmness. Nothing unreasonable was ever going to be asked. On the headset, well, anything goes. The game is so fast paced, you have to be a part of it to understand.

I can remember one time when George Henshaw wanted to run a particular play, and my dad wanted to run something else. They got into a little heated disagreement, and Dad said, "If this doesn't work, you're fired!"

It was a fake toss sweep play, where the runner throws the ball back to the tight end on the other side—one of those kind of deals. And it didn't work.

Well, I assumed George was going to be fired at the end of the game. But George said, "Oh no, he's done that to me several times." He never took it personally.

I never really coached for anybody else but him. I had one eight-month period at Akron with Gerry Faust in 1986. He was the only guy I trained in front of prior to getting my next head coaching job at Samford University in Birmingham.

I was not at Florida State when Wayne McDuffie was the offensive coordinator, but I always remember Dad saying how tough Wayne was on players. Wayne didn't make the game enjoyable, and Dad had to handle that with players.

There's one true story I heard that is just incredible. During a game at FSU, McDuffie just left the coaches' box—walked out. I guess he disagreed with some of the play calling Dad wanted, and he just left.

I mean, it's incredible. People can't believe that it's true that the guy walked out of the stadium and walked down the street to go home while the game was being played, but it happened. That's unbelievable. But Dad didn't get angry when he later found out about it.

My father wasn't very famous when I was growing up. He was an assistant coach at West Virginia for four years before he became the head coach in 1970.

That's when I would go to games and sit there around people who didn't know who I was, and all they would talk about is my dad. I guess that was my first real insight into what it was going to be like, that it was going to be a point of comment among people.

When he came to Florida State in 1976 and then the team went undefeated in 1979, that's when I saw the celebrity part of his role. There was a lot of attention. I sensed it was now a little more than him being just a football coach.

Back then, I don't think there were long-term contracts anywhere. I do remember how precarious his situation was after the 1974 season, when West Virginia finished 4-7.

I don't think it dawned on me that Dad getting fired was a possibility. I do know this: our lifestyle did not change financially from the standpoint of when he was an assistant at West Virginia until he was a head coach. We had the same house, never left. We didn't change our allowances or the amount of toys we had. We didn't have boats; we didn't get a lot of things.

Our lifestyle never changed, but I never felt the real pressure other than I knew people were after him and I heard it. We knew there were some mad people and it might cost him his job. But it never hit me like, "Oh no, what's he's going to do?" I never felt that way.

When he became a head coach at West Virginia, I was either in eighth grade or ninth grade. From that point, all I ever wanted to do was become a head coach. I had always liked sports, but I guess I didn't know until the ninth grade that I wasn't going to grow very big. In seventh or eighth grade, everybody shot past me.

The one thing that always struck me about Dad was how he fit in his desire to be actively involved in church. When he was the head coach at West Virginia, he was also an interim pastor at a church in Clarksburg, West Virginia, which was about 35 miles away from Morgantown, where the WVU campus is located and where we lived.

One year, every Saturday, we'd go to a game, and I would get in the car with him, and he would end up having to prepare a sermon, because he was an active pastor.

We were Southern Baptists. This church in Clarksburg was kind of like one of our mission churches. When we went to Morgantown, there were so few Southern Baptists that we met in a carpenter's union hall with about six other families.

Now, think about this: How many coaches would do that? How many would be a Sunday morning preacher, especially in their first years as a head coach? Think of all the things a head coach has to do on Sundays, too. And Dad would actually have to prepare a sermon and preach until the church eventually got a full-time preacher.

That really impressed me a lot. It has all my life, because I can't think of another coach who would do it. I don't know how Dad did it. He was 40-something years old at the time. I would have been scared to death. I would have been so focused on doing my job it would never have dawned on me that I could take another type of responsibility at the same time.

He had the sense of purpose to mix his faith and his office responsibilities, to mix his faith with his passion to be a football coach. He's pulled it off. Whether anyone agrees with it or not, he's pulled it off.

Now, I'm a big believer in the separation of church and state. My father and I talk about that a lot. We debate it. We talk about it on the radio show. But he feels strong enough to be able to mix the two, and he's going to do it.

THE DISCIPLINE ISSUE

What's misunderstood about my father? I think his whole philosophy on discipline is probably misunderstood. You have to take the total picture from when he first started to where he is now.

To us, as children, he was always very firm but always very fair. I think the people who think he's a lax disciplinarian don't understand how important it is to him for kids to do right instead of wrong and to know good from bad.

I think some coaches, for example, will run a player on stadium steps because he missed practice but then don't really care what happens to the player in all other aspects of his life. My father is not that way. He cares about the total person beyond football. I think the criticism he gets on discipline is very overstated.

To any college coach, and I went through this myself, it's easier to overdiscipline than to underdiscipline. When you overdiscipline, your boosters jump up and down happily and clap and pat you on the back, and the media write good stuff about you. If you're insecure or you really haven't found your mark in coaching, it's always easier to discipline.

I think Dad has always tried to be fair. He has treated his players like he treated his children. There was much more fairness involved, a much more rational way of dealing with things in his mind. But most people don't understand that.

People use their own rationale. Many of them believe you play a guy because winning is the most important thing in your life. I think Dad looks at it, and says, "OK, I've been coaching for a long time. I know what I'm doing."

Remember, there was no Internet back in the 60s. The media weren't around the program every minute like they are now, and my father remembers how he would run a kid in the morning and play a football game in the afternoon. That's how we all dealt with it.

Somewhere along the line, as it is now, it has evolved to being something like, "OK, you need to suspend a guy for this, suspend a guy for that." I think Dad believes winning is a team concept, and there are a lot of people who suffer when you remove a player. There are other ways to deal with things.

If he thought he was going to lose a kid spiritually or lose a kid's morals or lose a kid to a tough environment, or if he thought not play-ing a kid would change that kid's life for the better, then he would do it. But he never saw it the same way some people see it.

I think he is very much like Tom Osborne in that regard. Think about this, two of the wisest, most respected, most moral men out there—two of the longest-lasting guys in college foot-ball—were both considered to be coaches who had no discipline—Bobby Bowden and Tom Osborne. There must be a parallel between them. Maybe it's having a lot of kids and understanding that everybody makes mistakes in his life, and we always end up being OK.

HURTING FOR A SON

Without question, the toughest thing my father has gone through has occurred in the last four or five years with my brother Jeff as the offensive coordinator. There is so much debate on this subject, and I get it all the time doing my radio show in Orlando. I hear all the comments and take the calls. And it's tough because it's my brother. To me, it's up to Dad to solve it.

Maybe I'm wrong on this, but if there is any one important thing that Dad has not done, he has not given Jeff what he has given all his other coordinators.

When I think of the system that Charlie Ward ran in 1992 and '93, well, Dad put that in. Tommy was a big influence on passing that along to Dad and me. Tommy was great about giving us ideas that he got from Homer Smith when the two worked together while Smith was offensive coordinator at Alabama.

But when Dad wanted to set an offensive style, he said, "This is what I want to run, and we're going to run it."

When he went to that West Coast offense at Florida State in the mid-'80s with Dexter Carter and split backs, and the quarterback under center, that was Dad's offense. He was exactly like, "This is what I want to do."

I don't think Jeff has ever gotten that. I think Jeff has never had that feeling from Dad that, "Jeff, you better run this." But I get the impression that in the off-season, Dad has gone back to that a little bit.

I think it's where, ultimately, Dad is responsible for the last five years.

That being said, I'm not going to jump ship on him. He's won too many games.

You have to keep in mind Florida State has had a very unusual quarterback situation. And it's been a quarterback situation without a different direction to go. It's not like they had another choice. Chris Rix did not develop like they wanted him to, but there weren't a whole lot of alternatives for those years from 2001 to '04. I think now they have the quarterback situation stabilized.

When Wyatt Sexton had to sit out last season, that was another setback. I think when you look back on last year, it will become a huge disappointment, but only because, again, they had to start a redshirt freshman quarterback in Drew Weatherford, who had to learn under fire.

I think when you see that only eight or nine players were drafted on FSU's team, which had 19 seniors, I think last year becomes an even bigger disappointment. But it's also the fifth year in a row that a strong upperclassman quarterback has not been there.

All that said, I do believe Dad has made his career by reinventing himself. You can start from 1979 and go on. He's been successful by reinventing himself throughout his career.

He went from toss-sweep style in '78 to the Veer Offense to the West Coast Offense in the mid-'80s to the no-huddle stuff in the early '90s. I think there has been that point in time since 2001 where Dad needed to reassert himself and reinvent that offense. I don't think there has been a real reinvention there.

I sense now that Dad has got some mandates in. I think he wants to run the football no matter what. This is just my opinion, but it's what I think he feels. I also think Dad's fed up with the criticism. He can handle stuff about himself, but when it's with Jeff, it is personal.

I would be the first to say you can't blame anybody. Because Jeff's his coordinator and his son, it's going to become personal. The lesson learned is when you name your son the coordinator, the first time things don't go right, you better realize people are going to say it's nepotism.

It seems unfair to Dad; he took it so personal. He wanted Jeff to get the same fair shake that everybody else got, but it hasn't worked out that way. He and the Chris Rix era came in together during those first four years.

To me, nothing has been as personal or as tough on Dad from a professional standpoint than having to deal with the way he perceives people are treating Jeff. He lives in the perception of the way people feel, and it has been pretty ugly. Jeff has handled it well. I think the only other time something this tough occurred was in 1974 at West Virginia, when Dad really felt like he was going to be fired.

I don't think fans or boosters at Florida State are any different now than they were 10 or 15 or 20 years ago. The fact is, the success hasn't been there the last four or five years the way it was before then. The bottom line is they haven't won as much.

I don't know that people's demands are out of line. I just think Dad wishes it were not so directed at Jeff, but that's the way it is. As long as Dad can take it and Jeff can take it, then people are going to have to yell. It's a tough situation.

If it were me, I think if I had to go back and do it again, if I were Jeff, I don't know if I would want to be a coordinator for Dad. And if I were Dad, I don't know if I would want Jeff as coordinator. Same with me as coordinator, or Tommy, or any of us. But Dad doesn't ever break down on that one. He'll say, "Well dang, we won the ACC," as they did last year.

The question is, at Dad's age—and he turns 77 in November—can he still rise to the occasion and make it happen? That's what the debate is right now. Can Dad make it happen? I believe he's totally in charge, but that's the debate. At 77, can he still get it done? If Joe Paterno can do it, so can my father. But that's the debate: can my dad get FSU to a championship level again?

DEATH OF A PLAYER

I had a player die when I was the head coach at Samford. There is nothing more difficult and heartfelt for a coach than to lose a player. And it certainly affected Dad when one of his own players, Devaughn Darling, died in 2001 during their off-season conditioning workouts known as mat drills. Anyone who knows my father knows that he has sincere concern and love for his players. The parents trust the coach with their sons.

One of the things coaches around the country talked about when they discussed Florida State and Dad was the mat drills, one of the program's trademarks. It was something that gave FSU the edge—that made them different and better. Plenty of coaches building their programs wanted to have mat drills like Florida State's. Without a doubt,

Devaughn's death made him reevaluate the mat drills and how they were handled.

A FATHER'S LEGACY

Over the years, I don't know anybody who has known how to handle the pressures of the media better than my father. He's in a different world, in that regard, than Joe Paterno. Joe doesn't do interviews half the time.

I think that aspect helped me through my situation when I left at Auburn as head coach in 1998. Dad stood very much behind me, but I don't think he understood what all was going on. I'm not sure anybody could. I'm not sure I did.

I know more now than I did then, and I had to do a lot of researching and soul-searching. But Dad stood by me. I said, "Dad, they're going to fire me at Auburn. I've got to walk away." Dad was very supportive. I know he heard all the junk that was going on about me.

He never encouraged me to get back into coaching, because he really never encouraged us to get into coaching in the first place. I think he'd say, "Terry, are you happy?"

I think if he thought I wasn't happy, he would say something. But it was clear after a year or two, outside of coaching, that I had gotten onto a different horse, so he was very supportive.

Right now it's hard to measure the impact my father has made at Florida State. I know this: I was a part of the experience when there were only 17,000 to 18,000 people watching games at Florida State, and 40,000 if it was a sellout. It was the sleepy, little school in a sleepy, little town. Whether Florida State could have grown like it has as a university by itself, I don't know.

I would have to say, at the very least, what my father has done has sure made everything else a lot easier. Everything else became a possibility when Florida State started to become so nationally well-known that people wanted to go there.

Dad has two national championships. I don't know if it's that second one that puts a coach into a different level or it's the third one. I think if you asked him, he would give up being the win-ningest coach in history for another national championship. I think championships are what drive him, to show he can do it one more time.

For me, when I look back on his career and think of those first years at West Virginia and the time he was a head coach and pastor on the side, you go from that into what I think my father should be remembered for. Without a doubt, I believe my father's legacy will be that he will have made an impact on the spiritual lives of young people more than any other coach in history.

You take any other coach in any other sport in history, and my father will have made a bigger spiritual impact on young people. And it's because of that intertwining commitment he had to his faith and to his sport. And it carried over from that very first time at West Virginia.

I also think he will be remembered as one of the greatest coaches of all time. I expect him to be the winningest Division I coach of all time. But I would like for him to be remembered as the coach who made the greatest impact on the spiritual life of young people.

Here's an example. At the church my family and I attend in Orlando, we got a new assistant pastor. After Easter service, as we were leaving the church to greet him, he grabbed me and said, "Terry, I just want you to know I was a student assistant at West Virginia when your dad was the head coach. And I wasn't a Christian, but he changed my life."

Now he's a minister for a congregation as large as 6,000 to 7,000 people. That's what I'm talking about. And this has happened over and over and over again.

It may be a Deion Sanders or a Mark Richt or someone else, but Dad has made a profound impact on the spirituality of others. That will be what Dad intended his life to be.

JEFF BOWDEN

As the youngest of Bobby Bowden's sons, Jeff Bowden was used to hard knocks. Whether it was backyard football, sibling horseplay, or the kid brother hand-me-downs, he had to scrap for everything. That continued throughout his teenage years. After his father accepted the Florida State head coaching position in 1976, Jeff joined the team as a walk-on receiver. He got to participate in three bowl games. After deciding to go into coaching, he joined older brother Terry on the staff at Salem College in West Virginia. Following a one-year stint in 1986 as a graduate assistant at FSU, he rejoined Terry at Samford University in Birmingham, Alabama—formerly Howard College—where Bobby Bowden had established himself from 1959 to 1962.

At Samford, Jeff Bowden became offensive coordinator, working with Jimbo Fisher, who became an NCAA Division III All-America quarterback in the Bulldogs' offense.

Jeff Bowden joined Florida State's staff as a receivers coach in 1994, following the Seminoles' first national title season. After the 2000 season, when Mark Richt was named head coach at Georgia, he was promoted to offensive coordinator. Watching his father deal with fan and media criticism throughout his career has served Jeff Bowden well in handling his well-scrutinized role as FSU's offensive coordinator.

When I was growing up, I never really thought about going into the coaching profession. That really didn't happen until I graduated from Florida State. There were other things I wanted to do, but I always knew coaching was out there for me, that I could go into it.

In college, I loved the idea of going into law enforcement—not so much at the local level, but the DEA, the Secret Service. As I got into studying the various aspects of law enforcement, the crime scene portion and the investigation area really interested me.

I couldn't get interested in desk jobs. I couldn't be inside all day and enjoy my life. I had to do something where I could interact. I guess that's what always attracted me to coaching. It wasn't until I neared graduation when I said, "Hey, it's time for me to make a decision."

Family beach vacations always gave Terry Bowden (arms folded, far left) a chance to share strategy with his brothers and father.
Courtesy of FSU Sports Information

The decision wasn't hard. That was just the way I was raised. It was more of a case of just making a decision, knowing I could always change my mind. But the reality of coaching is that it's better to make that choice early before you get married, before you have children, to find out if you like it and if you're committed to it. If you want to change after going into coaching, that part is easy.

I knew what I liked about coaching. It was a different level of camaraderie, a different level of interaction with kids. You're a little more of a teacher. Early on, it was just nothing but coaching, just teaching football. But as I have gotten older, I've tried to teach them more things than just football.

I didn't really study my father's coaching style when I was growing up. It probably was not until we moved to Tallahassee that I paid more attention to what he did as a coach. Really, at West Virginia, I wasn't paying attention. I played football and loved it. I played all the sports and loved them all. My focus was not watching him, not trying to learn at a young age what the heck he was doing.

I don't think any of the things he did in coaching were the biggest things I admired about him. I think, just like a fan, I saw how big those things like the great victory we had over Florida in 1977 are, but they still weren't the things I admired in him. In fact, it wasn't anything about his career.

I admired just the way he was, the way he carried himself, the way he worked. Every morning I would wake up, and his routine was the same. He was going to read his newspaper; he was going to read a daily spiritual message; he was going to read his Bible; and then he was going to read the comics in the newspaper. Every morning growing up, same thing. He drank a cup of coffee, then out the door.

Then every Sunday we were in church. Every other Sunday, it seemed, he was either drawing plays on the program or you could watch his head nod off because you knew he had worked late the night before. But there was a routine with him.

It's what we've always said; what you see is what you get with him. He had a certain lifestyle he lived—he brought his family up like that. He never wavered. He was never desensitized throughout the years. What he believed 25 years ago he still believes today.

He had no say in me going into coaching. I never went to him for an opinion. He just said, "If you're going in it, start as a GA, a graduate assistant." There was a graduate assistant opening at FSU when I graduated.

I could have done that, but I knew it wasn't wise, because I was a little bit of a hellion. For me to go out and coach and talk about discipline when I wasn't that way myself, and try to coach players I had been friends with two seasons before would have been foolish.

So the best thing was to get the heck out of Dodge, try to straighten up a little bit, and get serious about coaching. My brother Terry was a graduate assistant here, then stayed on as a volunteer assistant, then took a head job at Salem College in West Virginia right from Florida State. That's when he invited me up for housing and meals, and he said, "I'll pay you as much as I can afford." That turned out to be about $150 a month on a nine-month contract.

For my housing, I was a resident assistant on the sixth floor of the boys dorm. My meals were on the training table. My supplemental salary was basically that I was a chaperone at the student union. There was no place to socialize in Salem. We did it on campus.

They had a dance every Friday night. I would be there every Friday just standing in the back supervising. They paid me $50 for that.

Growing up, I don't think my father's so-called celebrity status began until he was at Florida State. That's when the success really started. When we first moved to Tallahassee in 1976, there was excitement over him, the new coach, coming to town.

But at West Virginia, we never really had that sense in our house. In our house, listening to conversations between Mom and Dad, I remember the talks about "Why do we only have a one-year contract?" I remember talks about salary. I remember talks about job security. It was a struggle up at West Virginia. And I probably remember more of that because big-win seasons didn't come nearly as often as they did at Florida State.

The first real big win was beating Florida at Florida in 1977, especially because of the way we won that game. That was the No. 1 mission—beating Florida, because Miami was not the Miami we know now.

FATHERLY ADVICE

My father hasn't changed the way he addresses coaches before the season. Back when he first started, I know he gave each coach a piece of paper with a list of the person's responsibilities. That is still going on today. That's something we go through in our coaches' hideaway every year. He hands us each a sheet of paper and lets us know what our responsibilities are. Every coach has a list of responsibilities.

Some coaches have larger responsibilities, but the duties are specific things throughout the course of the year. As a coach, you are required to make sure that you take care of it. Some of these duties apply to every coach, but some are specific. He goes through each one before the season begins.

I think everybody who works for Dad kind of understands the lifestyle he expects you to live to a certain degree. You don't have to be just like him, but he doesn't like a lot of stuff out in the public. If you're out there flaunting it, drinking, or chasing women, he'll let you go.

He's given me advice all through the years. One was to play golf, because the type of people I was going to meet were going to play golf, so it was a great way to socialize and get to know people. The best piece of advice he's ever given me is "Be yourself," because I think he knows how all of us, all the children, admired him and wanted to emulate him, and that's not the way to go into coaching.

And I've gone through that. There have been times I've tried to be like him, and it's just not me. It's going to come across as phony or fake, so that was good advice. That's the best advice I think you can give anybody, just on how to coach.

Other than that, his advice to me is the same as he would give any coach. He presents the bottom line in football: "This is what you have to do to win." You can talk about all the gadget plays and this or that, but it comes down to blocking and tackling, things like that. And he hasn't changed. Those are notes he has every year, aspects he is truly adamant about, and he's truly right.

I don't know if I got this from him, but I love to watch film, just as he does. It doesn't bother me to sit in a room and just watch film, not just our team or our opponent, but just to watch film of other teams to see what they're doing. I compare us to them. Are we doing "this" as good as them? Are our backs running as hard? Are our receivers going through routes as hard as another team? I enjoy that.

Dad will lock himself in his office until lunchtime, and he'll sit there with his feet up on his desk, watching film the whole time. It amazes me he does that at his age. You would think at some point he would say, "I've seen this stuff a hundred times." But he loves doing it, and he does it at home.

When I played under him, as a receiver, the thing I liked best was his pregame and halftime talks. And they haven't changed all these years. But I can distinctly remember as a player how fired up he made me feel to want to go out and play. Get after it and play. That was something. I don't know if anybody can emulate it, because everybody has their own style. But if there was something I wish I could copy from him, I wish I could do that.

He would make us sit on the edge of our seats and just want to go punch somebody, just want to go play football. I really remember that. It wasn't just his tone. He had good messages. He had different challenges, but it was more about the passion. We could just feel it and know he meant it. The talks have changed a little bit throughout the years, and a lot of them are the same to the coaches, but the players change.

I can imagine they feel the same way as I did a long time ago. As a player, he didn't treat me any different. I remember my freshman or sophomore year I decided I didn't want to do a lot of studying. I came home with bad grades one semester, so he yanked me out of the dorm. He made me move home the next semester. It was the most miserable I've ever been. I went from having freedom to having no freedom. He was there every morning, so I couldn't stay out late. It was a case of too much partying and not enough going to school and doing what I was supposed to do in school, so he made me move home.

Number one, it's embarrassing. Your teammates are calling, "Where are you at?" And I had to say, "I'm home with Mom and Dad."

The other thing was I was not on scholarship when I decided to attend Florida State. He said, "Look, if you choose to play football, I'll pay for your education. But if you're not going to be involved with it, you're going to get a job." He wasn't going to let me or any of us go to college and have all that free time. I wanted to play football anyway. I wanted to see if I could make it. So that part wasn't difficult. But I knew I had to bear down.

He never gave us an allowance. So it wasn't like he could take money away. We had none. If we wanted money, he would tell us to get a job. I did get some hand-me-downs, like an old used car that one of my brothers had gotten from a grandmother.

His expectations were pretty simple. It's the same expectations he tells players today. All he wants for them to do is the best they can do.

He just wanted us to do what we were capable of doing. His whole philosophy was "Don't start something—whether it's school, football, getting a job, or starting a fight—unless you plan on finishing it." He'll say the same thing to players. He doesn't expect all 85 players to be A or B students. He wants them to do the best they can and everything they are asked to do.

DECIDING TO WORK ON MY FATHER'S STAFF

When a coaching position opened at Florida State, as receivers coach, it was something I had to do. I had to jump at this opportunity to work with Dad. It went back to what my brothers Terry and Tommy said to me—that they regretted never having the opportunity to work with him. That's why I said, "Man, I've got to have this chance." Whether it was going to last two, three, five years, whatever. I wanted that opportunity. I had no idea that I would be going into my 13th season in 2006 on this staff, but it's been everything I hoped it would be.

My father is no different dealing with coaches than he was dealing with us growing up. If you ask the other coaches, that's what makes him different than a lot of head coaches. He doesn't belittle coaches. He doesn't pull rank unless he has to.

I think if you ask any of the other coaches, they would say that Dad has a way of suggesting something that we understand as "You better change." That's his way of saying, "Don't do it your way, do it my way."

Some head coaches will get into a meeting room and rip you and tear you down and say, "Look, this is what we're going to do." He's never been that way. It's not just with me. He's never been that way with any of his coaches.

No matter what happens on Saturday, win or lose, you always have to start preparing for the next game the very next day. That's always been his outlook. Don't live in yesterday, there's always another one to get ready for. The toughest thing about working for him, that I can say, is not succeeding for him. That's the toughest thing for me.

He's the kind of guy that you don't want to fail for. You want to do it for him. There are not a lot of coaches in your lifetime like him whom you get to work for. There are a lot of SOBs out there whom you don't want to work for. He makes an extremely tough profession enjoyable. He makes going to work enjoyable. It's just not always that way with other coaches.

We've had some pretty good exchanges during a game. I can remember a game we had against Duke in 2003, and we were in one of those running modes. We ran a play for Lorenzo Booker, and he ran for about 20 or 30 yards. I thought he could have gotten more yards. I sat there in the press box and mumbled all these bad words like dadgum dancing, juking, and all that.

Dad yelled on the headset, "Why don't you just shut up! I like the way he runs."

I can sympathize with Mark Richt, who was the offensive coordinator. Mark was a big shotgun guy because he knew that as soon as the players line up in the I-formation, they were in Bobby Bowden's world. That's his game, lining up in the I-formation. Mark made us so successful in the shotgun.

The last few seasons, as we have lost more games than we're used to losing, it hasn't been any different with Dad. When we lose games, it eats at every one of us. We're not into moral victories. We're not into close losses. We're beyond that. I'm sure it really eats at him, but as the leader, he can't sit there and be down in front of us. He's got to be the guy who pushes us on, and that's exactly the way he has been.

When we get a new assistant coach, that's what they emphasize— that they haven't been around a guy like Dad. He's unbelievable in the way he handles the team. And there's stuff coming at him from a lot of different directions. But he's shown a lot of true strength.

I think there are some things he's gotten fed up with. He's finally drawn a line in the sand and said, "I've had enough of some of this stuff." A lot of that has to do with media coverage or the way fans act.

You know he's always had that good-old-boy nature, that philosophy of "What's said is said, what's done is done, and we'll just go on." But what people have seen a little bit in the last few years is that he has drawn that line. There are some things he's tired of and won't put up with. And without being specific about it, I think people know what I'm talking about.

The things that have changed now is not so much the traditional media, but nowadays you have the Internet, the message boards, all of that. It's a whole other outlet. I've come to the conclusion that we're just in a cycle of the way things get reported.

A LASTING LEGACY

The thing that flat-out irritates me, the thing I've heard for 15 years, is that Dad's not a disciplinarian. The best way I've heard that perception refuted is that he treats every case individually. He has always felt like he did not want 84 teammates to suffer for the mistake of one.

Our placekicker, Sebastian Janikowski, was late for curfew when we were in New Orleans in 1999 preparing to play Virginia Tech in the Sugar Bowl for the national championship. Dad could have suspended him right there, and the whole team would have suffered because of a curfew violation, but Dad didn't think it was fair to punish the whole team.

The one thing about his discipline is when it was done it was done. When we stepped out of line as children, we got a whipping. But from that point on, we moved on. I have heard people make comments that he has no discipline over the players. That is the most asinine thing I have ever heard.

There are times when he's not around the team or the players, but he expects the coaches to be around. That's our job. Let me tell you, he's always aware of what's happening. It's not like he doesn't know what's going on.

I think his legacy as a coach is very similar to his legacy as a father. He's been successful at both. He's adapted through generations of players. He's stayed pretty much the same. He's made changes, but he's learned to adapt and make changes in his life to fit society, to fit our age.

I think he's going to be remembered in two different areas. I think there's an entire community that is going to recognize him for what he is as a man, a father, a leader, and an example in this community, throughout the world. Then I think there are people who are going to recognize him for what he did athletically, in coaching.

For me, the biggest thing is what he's been as a man. It's all the qualities he's been as a man, the foundation he's lived by, the fact he has never wavered in his beliefs. Those are the values that have made him successful. It is what I will always admire him for and why I think he's the greatest coach.

CHUCK AMATO

---◄•═══◄○►═══•►---

THE UNDERSTUDY

When Chuck Amato joined Bobby Bowden's coaching staff at Florida State in 1982, he filled an immediate need for a recruiter in the Miami-Dade County region. Amato later joked that the assignment was the result of drawing straws or that his east-Pennsylvanian accent made him a natural fit to blend into Miami's diverse culture. But the truth was Amato eagerly accepted that area to recruit, knowing how many talented high school players resided in the heavily populated area.

He clicked with Miami prep coaches the same way he clicked with Bowden. It was part of Amato's can-do style at FSU. He spent 18 seasons under Bowden, 14 of them as assistant head coach, working directly on a variety of important roles. Following the Seminoles' undefeated national title season in 1999, Amato accepted the head coaching job at NC State, returning to his alma mater.

In 2001, he led the Wolfpack to an upset win in Tallahassee, becoming the first visiting ACC team to win at Doak Campbell Stadium. Two other wins against the Seminoles have since followed. Passing years have not changed the emotional aspect of working at FSU for Amato, who still visits Tallahassee during the off-season and communicates with Bowden weekly during the season.

You know those secretarial notepads with spiral tops? I've got a pad for every year I was at Florida State—all 18 years. I still go back and look at those pads. That's what working under Coach Bowden did for me.

I'd keep the notes from our hideaway sessions, which were the coaches' retreats before the season. I kept practice notes, daily notes, and devotional notes. It's amazing how so much would be similar from year to year.

I would also sit in offensive meetings as much as I could, but that was tough because we were also in our own meetings. I wanted to learn what was going on in the offensive coaches' heads because I always felt I had to know offensive philosophy and theory to be a good defensive coach.

So all of that knowledge I absorbed during my time at Florida State was big. And the blueprint I brought to NC State was, to a T, like the one I learned under Coach Bowden.

What I think I take from him and what people perceive I took from him are not necessarily the same. I know the way he handled the media; he was so media-friendly. And when I came to NC State, I met with media, and I joked, and I tried to have a good time with 'em, or at least tried to. And 95 percent of the media liked it, because I wasn't stiff-necked and I would be as honest as I could be. I might give the answers people want to hear, but I can answer the same question a month from now the same way. That's what I've tried to take from Coach Bowden.

When I was at Florida State, being at banquets with Coach Bowden, being at booster functions with him, the booster caravan, the golf tour in April and May, how he handled people—all of that I took from him.

I can remember one of the first times I was with him on a booster meeting in Miami. Somebody stood up and said, "When are we going to sign a big-name quarterback?" That year, I had personally recruited Mike Shula, whom Alabama wasn't recruiting at the time; Mark Maye from North Carolina; and Danny McManus. We ended up getting Danny McManus.

Well, Coach Bowden looked at this guy, who was standing up, and told him: "Who's to say we didn't sign the best quarterback out there?" He didn't even hesitate to answer it.

You could almost feel just a little bit of undertow, some edge in his answer, but there was that twinkle in his eye when he said, "Who's to say we didn't sign the best quarterback?" So the guy had to sit down.

That's Coach Bowden. He's been around so much. He knows how to handle every situation. He adjusts to all that stuff. He never shows anger.

You can tell there are times when he doesn't like this or that—whether it's media-related, or whatever—but he'll never say it. I would just marvel at how he would stay with his demeanor because he's a tough man. A lot of that comes from his faith. If he was hurt, and I'm sure he was at times, he didn't show it.

MAINTAINING RELATIONSHIPS

As for dealing with players, that was always something I felt like I was good at. I had to do a lot of discipline at Florida State, but I feel like I have a knack with kids. I can deal with young people, and I enjoy dealing with them. I always learned to just be honest with kids, which is what Coach Bowden did. I think it all has do with being honest with a kid and establishing that trust factor between the two. That's not easy to get. Coach Bowden is able to get it.

In my first six years as head coach at NC State, I lost 12 coaches. I only fired one. To me, that's a compliment. It was not like I was losing coaches to smaller schools. I was losing them to the NFL, to the University of Southern California, or to a Southeastern Conference school for $100,000 more than they were making here, and they were making good money here at NC State. But I got criticized for losing coaches, and naturally it started to get me worried about what I was doing.

After my third season, I called Coach Bowden and talked to him about that. I said, "Coach, I conduct meetings like we did there at Florida State, and yet the word *intimidation* gets out when my name is involved on why I am losing coaches." I asked, "Why? I haven't screamed or hollered. I haven't hit anybody."

Coach Bowden listened, and then he said, "Chuck, when I first got here, I averaged losing about two coaches a year until maybe

After 18 years as an FSU assistant, NC State head coach Chuck Amato (R), shown meeting with Bobby Bowden prior to a game between the teams, has maintained a warm relationship with him. *Courtesy of FSU Sports Information*

when you got here and we started that long run of success. So it will settle down, because the grass always looks greener on the other side to people, and you don't know 'em all when you hire them, but sooner or later, it will all fit in and you'll be able to put it all together."

That advice meant a lot to me.

During my time at Florida State, I kept asking Coach Bowden for more responsibilities. I think that's why I kept adding responsibilities. I'd say, "Coach, go enjoy playing golf. You've earned the right to do all that stuff, and we can handle this or handle that." Shows he's a smart man, doesn't it? No, I'm just kidding. But I think I earned his trust the first couple years, and he saw how I dealt with problems and with kids and with staff.

Tommy Bowden would say to me, "You're the first person Dad gave so much rein to." I think it's the trust he had in me.

My office was next to his for 14 of the 18 years I was there. So I was close to him, literally and figuratively. But in last six years since I became head coach at NC State, I've become even closer to him. I call him once a week, at least, during the season—even the week when we're going to play them.

Sometimes I call him more than once a week. He always says, "If you need me, call me." It's such a relief to know that. He's also said, "When you want to come back, call me too," but it's all in jest.

FIRST MEETING WITH BOWDEN

The first time I met Coach Bowden was in the 1972 Peach Bowl, when he was the head coach at West Virginia. I was a graduate assistant at NC State. Lou Holtz was the head coach. Back then, the Peach Bowl had a lot of team functions. The teams got together for either two luncheons and a dinner, or two dinners and a luncheon.

We wound up winning the game big, 49–13. In that game, West Virginia was favored to win. We played them again in the 1975 Peach Bowl, which was Coach Bowden's last game at West Virginia. We were supposed to win, but they beat us 13–10. I was the secondary coach at the time at NC State. I would have bet my house we were going to win that game.

I've been very blessed. I got my start in coaching under Lou Holtz as a full-time assistant, then I spent 18 years working under Bobby Bowden at Florida State. They're both winners, and they're different. Fundamentals are the very essence of their programs, and attitude is the way they changed attitudes.

Talk about timing—I left NC State and was at the University of Arizona in 1980 and '81. The other defensive coaches and I went to visit the Tampa Bay Buccaneers and their defensive staff. One of their defensive coaches used to be a coordinator at UCLA, and we knew him. We looked at the map and said, "Well, since we're that close, let's stay the whole week in Florida, spend a couple days in Tampa, then drive up to Tallahassee and watch Florida State's spring practice."

At the time, Jack Stanton was the defensive coordinator at Florida State. I had worked under him as a graduate assistant at NC State before he went to Florida State the first time. He came back when Coach Bowden was hired.

While our staff was in Tallahassee that spring, Jack asked me if I would be interested in coming there as a coach.

I said, "Well, you don't have an opening."

He said, "It looks like we might."

So he must have said something to Coach Bowden, because he wanted to meet me. I chatted with Coach Bowden for about 30 or 40 minutes and went home and didn't think anything of it. It was probably about a month later when I got a call from FSU and was presented the job offer.

I called Coach Holtz and Norm Sloan, who was the head basketball coach at Florida at the time, for advice. I knew Coach Sloan, of course, from his time at NC State.

Coach Sloan said to me, "If you have a chance to go to Florida State and work with that Bobby Bowden fellow, do it. That guy has got his act together. He's good. You need to take that job."

Then I talked with Coach Holtz, and I'll never forget this: It was a Sunday. The talk was that I was going to be offered a job working at Arkansas under Coach Holtz as the linebackers coach. One way or the other, I was leaving, because if I didn't go to Florida State, I couldn't turn down Lou another time.

He said, "Chuck, I'm going to give you three questions: What was your first gut feeling when they asked you? How does your family feel about it? And where can you win the most games right now?"

He said, "You call me when you make the choice."

Arizona tried to talk me out of it in a lot of different ways, but leaving for Florida State was the greatest decision I'd ever made in my life.

SUCCESS BEFORE RESOURCES

I came to Florida State as the defensive line coach, but it didn't really matter what responsibilities I had. I always thought defensive line was the most boring position in the world to coach. But I realized after coaching it that you have to have a great line coach on both sides of the ball, and you have to have good players.

Pass rushers became such a big thing because all of a sudden, college football went from option football to passing football. I didn't care where I was going to go recruiting. I didn't really care. I think we drew straws, and I got the Miami area.

From people I knew in Pennsylvania, I heard about what Coach Bowden had done at West Virginia, how he built that program there. So my respect for him was right off the bat. Sitting down with him only reinforced it.

He just seemed like such a genuine individual. I was kind of in awe sitting in his office. You can imagine what that office looked like. It didn't take me long to say, "He's going to be somebody special."

I think I was always concerned about making moves. I didn't want to be a journeyman. My first couple years at FSU, I was offered jobs, which nobody knew about, but I chose to stay. I only looked into one job. Being there and seeing what Coach Bowden had already done made me think the program was going to be a big-time program.

Usually, when you build a program, most people have to build facilities, brick and mortar, which seems silly, but that's how it is—and then the program comes. But at Florida State, they built the program, and then they built facilities. So I said, "What kind of potential does this place have?"

I think one of the biggest things that impressed me was the fact that, on the field, Coach Bowden let the coaches coach. He gave people responsibility, and it was understood they would do what was expected. We would sit down at our hideaway, our coaches' retreat before the season, and he would read over everybody's responsibilities in front of everybody. It was like, "Do your job, and if you've got a problem, come and see me, but I hope you can resolve it individually or collectively as a group."

On the field, he let the coaches coach. The next morning in our staff meetings, he would correct things that he thought needed to be looked at.

He's so professional. He was a breath of fresh air compared to other coaches.

For some reason, I always sat opposite of him at staff meetings. He could chew you out with a twinkle in his eye. And you would leave that thing and say, "You know what? Coach Bowden just chewed my butt out." And you realized, if you were smart enough to realize it, "I need to do something about this or that." But I don't ever remember him embarrassing a coach. He was respectful to everybody and to all people, including the media.

He was professional in the way he handled coaches from other schools when you knew deep down he wanted to say something bad about Coach So-and-so from School So-and-so. But he would never do it. I remember thinking, "Wow, he is such a strong individual."

I remember in 1989, we went 0-2 at Florida State, losing to Southern Miss and Clemson. I remember one of my daughters said, "Does this mean we won't go to a bowl?" Oh man. Now, it's funny; at the moment, it was not.

But as for Coach Bowden, the meter never changed. On Monday morning, no matter if it was that circumstance or another, it was going to be like this from him:

"I don't want to hear anything from y'all about another play, or offense, or defense, or if we did this, or if we did that.

"I'm going to tell you right now, all we have to do is tackle better, block better. Call the same game and we win. It all has to do with blocking or tackling." And he was so right.

I think a lot of times he might have been better in defeat, knowing a leader has to really stand up, because everybody is looking toward the leader.

HAVING TO COACH AGAINST BOWDEN

I guess the most emotional I got when having to play against Florida State was the game in 2001 in Tallahassee that we wound up winning 34–28. No one from the ACC had ever won against them in Tallahassee. It became a great game, and we had the lead when they made one last drive. I saw the ball thrown by Chris Rix on the last play of the game, and I couldn't tell whether it was a catch or not, so I looked at the stands.

I said to myself, "If the fans in that end zone stand up and cheer, we just lost. If they don't say a word, it's an incompletion."

I saw the fans didn't stand up. I said to my coaches in the press box, "What happened?" They said, "We just won." Well, I knew that, but I wanted to find out what had happened on the play. So I took those headphones off and jumped up in the air. It was a vertical jump—the biggest I ever had—about two and a half inches off the ground.

I walked across the field, and I saw Coach Bowden coming toward me with his security guard, Billy Smith, right behind him.

I was thinking, "What am I going to say to Coach Bowden? I mean, what do I say: 'Good game?' 'Better luck next year?' What do I say to the man who I worked under for 18 years, after winning a game like this?

He was his typical self. He said, "Chuck, that was a great game."

Well, as soon as he started to speak, I broke down. I was crying.

He said, "Chuck, what are you crying for? You ought to be happy."

I said, "Coach, I'm Italian, and when we're happy, we cry." But I didn't know what to say. As we broke off, I kept looking back, and Coach Bowden said, "Hey, I'll call you on Tuesday. Congratulations."

And you know what? On Tuesday that next week, he called me and we chatted and chatted.

Then we won again the following year at NC State, and that was just as tough. We had our fans running around all over the field, and I was worried somebody would say or do something. So I wanted to make sure he got off the field OK.

It's very difficult to coach against him. What I've tried to do is take it like we're scrimmaging in the fall or spring—just like it would be at Florida State—and I still have garnet and gold on. It's like a game where I envision he's got half the team and I've got the other half.

I think I know by sitting in the meetings and sitting in all the pregame meetings on Friday nights what kind of questions he was going to ask of everybody on the staff.

But every time we play Florida State, it's tough.

I remember standing on the field at Doak Campbell Stadium before the game in 2003 with Todd Stroud, who was our strength coach at the time and is now my defensive line coach. He played nose-guard for me at Florida State. I said, "Todd, look at this place. Look at that football center. Look at these stands. Look at all these people. This is amazing. It is absolutely amazing."

And then, what a game that was. It was another wild and woolly game. We missed an extra point and a chip-shot field goal during the game, and it went into overtime. If we had not missed those kicks, we might have beaten Florida State three years in a row.

But in overtime, they scored and we scored. We got into the second overtime period, and we had fourth-and-3. The coaches started to send the field goal unit on the field, and I said no. I called a time-out.

My feeling was that I had one of the best quarterbacks in America, if not *the* best quarterback, in Philip Rivers. He'd already thrown for about 400 yards. I had a kicker who had already missed an extra point and a field goal. I wasn't going to send him on the field in overtime. I'd rather win or lose with Philip.

But lo and behold, a walk-on linebacker, Allen Augustin, whom I recruited and brought to Florida State, made the play to deflect the pass away from our receiver, Jerricho Cotchery. If he had caught the ball, we might have scored. Florida State went on to win the game in two plays. Leon Washington scored on a running play.

When I met Coach Bowden at midfield, I said, "Coach, I'm probably going to get my butt ripped for what I did, but I truly believe, being around you for as long as I have, that was the only way to go—to put the ball in my best players' hands."

Coach Bowden said, "I'll help you." And he did. He stuck up for me and called me. That meant a lot too.

It's very hard to coach against him. But once the game starts, I can truly say I don't notice him as much as I watch the other coaches. But it's not just him, it's all the other coaches who make it tough on me. I know the equipment man at Florida State, the trainers, the administration. The relationships I had with all those coaches is so strong. It goes further than Coach Bowden. It's everybody.

Looking back on my years working with Coach Bowden, I was like a sponge around him. Sometimes that can wear out, but I don't think it ever wore out for me. When I think of Coach Bowden's legacy, I think of a coach who not only won the most games in history, but he won the right way. It shows you, it's sometimes all about timing, about being in the right place at the right time.

Coach Bowden has won with integrity. He is a professional. He started his coaching career at a time when the coaches were professionals, when there was a special dignity to the game. And when you walked across the field and shook somebody's hand, you were friends again. The game was over, no hard feelings, whether you won or lost. From that standpoint, it has changed so much.

But to see him being able to adjust to all that shows just how smart of an individual he really, really is—and how tough he is, inwardly. But most of all, it shows you how great of a coach he is.

MARK RICHT

———◆◈◉◈◆———

THE CONVERTED ONE

Mark Richt's resume was brief. He had been a backup quarterback to Jim Kelly at Miami, and he had just one year of coaching experience. But Bobby Bowden liked what he had heard about the aspiring coach, and he respected Richt's college coach, Howard Schnellenberger. That was enough for Richt to begin his tutelage under Bowden in 1985 as a graduate assistant. Richt spent 15 years at Florida State, and during that time he coached Heisman Trophy winners Charlie Ward and Chris Weinke and studied the art of trick plays from a master. In his seven years as FSU's offensive coordinator, Richt's offense finished among the top five nationally in scoring five times.

The knowledge gleaned at Florida State helped him earn SEC Coach of the Year in 2002 and 2005 at the University of Georgia, where he became the head coach in 2001. In 2002 he led the Bulldogs to their first SEC championship in 20 years. Richt has since added a second SEC title, and in January 2006 was awarded the Grant Teaff Coach of the Year award from the Fellowship of Christian Athletes. Also attending that banquet was Bobby Bowden, the man who in 1986 helped him receive Jesus Christ.

During the 1986 season, on an open date before playing North Carolina, offensive lineman Pablo Lopez had gone to a party on our campus. He was shot and killed. The next day, Coach Bowden had a team meeting, and I was there, keeping the doors closed so it would be private. I stood in the back of the room as Coach Bowden addressed the team about what had happened with Pablo. Coach started to talk about eternity, and he said he wasn't sure where Pablo was at that moment. Coach Bowden didn't know where Pablo was in regard to his faith, so he spelled out his beliefs to the players and he spelled out the Gospel.

Then the most poignant moment I remember from that meeting took place when Coach pointed to an empty seat where Pablo could have been sitting, and he said, "Men, you are 18 to 22 years old, and you think you are going to live forever. Pablo believed that too. Now he is gone. If that would have been you last night instead of Pablo, do you know where you would spend eternity?"

I was there in the back of the room, listening. He was talking to the players, and I just happened to be in the room, but he was speaking to me. All the memories came back to me from the time I had spent during my junior year in college, when I had a roommate, John Peasley, who had presented the Gospel of Jesus Christ to me. Because of things like peer pressure and not really understanding what the decision to become a Christian was about, I didn't want to be a hypocrite, and I figured there were things in my life that I wouldn't change.

While I listened to Coach, all the memories came back from the time I spent with John Peasley, and I became very convinced at that moment that then was the time for me to live for Christ and to accept the gift of his blood for my sins and to live for him. At the end of the meeting, Coach Bowden said, "Men, if any of you here want to talk to me about anything like this, my door is always open."

That night I knew that the next day I was going to go to his office and talk to him about it. I knew I wanted to pray to receive Christ, and that's what I did. I went in there and said, "Coach, I know you were speaking to the players, but I hope you don't mind if a young coach comes in and talks to you about it." And he said, "Sure, buddy."

He led me to the Lord right there, and I prayed to receive Christ as my Lord and Savior right there in the room. It was a very heartfelt decision and was a total change of my mind-set. At that moment, I knew I was saved and that I was going to begin the journey to try to live for him, and of course, that process is called sanctification. I've been working on that ever since. That was a huge milestone in my life.

Before that, I already had respect for Coach Bowden and appreciated the way he ran the program and did it with integrity. When I first started coaching, I had doubts as to whether coaching was for me, and my greatest causes of concern were the rumors about how recruiting top athletes may be a crooked business. You just hear horror stories. I was very apprehensive about being a coach, mainly for that reason. I loved the strategy and the Xs and Os, and the competition was very exciting to me. I was just concerned about how the business was run.

I can tell you as a guy who has been on the very inside, Coach Bowden always does things with integrity and with the best interest of the players at heart. He also cared very much about his coaching staff and our families. He provided a lot of stability for me in a very unstable profession. He gave me a chance in 1985 to coach the quarterbacks as a graduate assistant and gave me a chance to ultimately become a coordinator, which propelled me into the situation I have here at Georgia. But none of those things compare to that day when I walked into his office after Pablo passed away.

THE MODEL WAS AT FLORIDA STATE

God has ordained us to provide for and love our families. You don't want your job to be so all-consuming that you lose that; everything would be in vain.

Coach Bowden was a tremendous example for me in that way, because he provided an atmosphere where we could nurture our families. When our children were young, we would try to carve out any time we could to be together, and it was the situation at Florida State that our families were welcome. We have that same thing at Georgia, where we have children running all over the place. We have family night, where the families and players eat together to let the players see the coaches in a light other than that of some guy breathing down their neck to do things right on the field. It's the same model as what we did at Florida State. That was very meaningful to me.

There were a lot of things we did at Florida State that were very meaningful that shaped my view and shaped my life and shaped me as a husband and father. I bought into everything that Coach Bowden had in place—hook, line, and sinker. I've been blessed because of it. And I want the same for our coaches, if they choose it. Like we did at Florida State, we have chapel services and devotions that are all voluntary for the guys. Nothing is mandatory.

WHEN BOWDEN IS AT HIS BEST

If we ever lost any game—any game you lose is big—I always felt like Coach Bowden was at his best from the standpoint of an assistant coach. He could have come in and browbeat everybody. We certainly corrected mistakes, and we looked deep into what happened and why, but in a real constructive way.

He always was more concerned about how the team felt and the morale of the team and the morale of the staff instead of how he felt. We could sense that he was highly disappointed in losing the game, but his concern was what we were going to do then to win the next time around—what we were going to do to make sure the team morale stayed positive. Those are the lessons where he would not say to his coaches, "This is how you do it." He just did it and lived it. And as a young coach, I watched him. That helped me a bunch here at Georgia, where I could very easily have felt sorry for myself because the head coach has to take questions after a loss and decide how he wants to handle them. Does he want to blame everybody else, or does he take the blame and responsibility and move on? I learned a lot from Coach Bowden in that regard.

There were times at Florida State when I would be frustrated. I think we kind of created a monster by scoring so many points and getting so many yards. If we didn't reach a certain level of style points, we felt like we had failed that day, even if we won 31–10. I would always say that night or the next day that if that's the worst I have to go through in my job, I have the best job in America.

Maybe it was just me or maybe I learned from observing Coach, but my reaction to the bad things I know are going to happen in a game has always been not to fret. Coach was always upbeat with the players—a positive motivator. My goal was always to find out where we were in a game and what we were going to do about our situation. If we lost 15 yards on a personal foul, I wouldn't fret as much as I would if it were, say, second and 25, and what were we going to do then?

Coach was that way. Even after a game we lost, Coach wouldn't blame anybody. He would say, "Let's correct mistakes and not allow them to happen again. Let's move forward. What can we do to make the rest of the season successful, and how can we paint a picture to motivate these players?" That's something I learned from him.

The other thing is that he would allow the staff to take over the play-calling responsibility, and play-calling was something he had done for years and years and years. I know it could not have been easy for him to turn over that responsibility, but he had enough faith in us to do it. That had a real positive effect on us to say, "Hey, I trust you to do this." Even when we were floundering away, he didn't get away from that approach. He just helped us grow and get better at play-calling.

I really didn't have any problem with who called the plays. If he wanted to say, "I want this series," then my response was, "You got it, Coach." If he wanted to take it over completely, I had no trouble with that. All I asked was that if I was calling the plays, just to allow me to keep my train of thought. And if we were going to have discussions, then let's have them in between series. I would approach him in a very respectful way—I was just trying to explain how I felt about him making suggestions during a series. He wasn't really browbeating or even being critical. I think he was just trying to help make suggestions on things to do. But during the middle of a series he would disrupt my train of thought, so I just made that known to him. I'd go to him maybe the next day or Monday and say, "I'll handle it any way you want to, but here's how I can do a better job for you."

Most of the time his reaction was kind of apologetic. He would say, "I'll stay out of your hair. I'm just trying to help. My intention wasn't to disrupt what you were doing. You're doing a good job." He was really gracious every time I ever approached him about that.

We just had to get used to each other. Coach Bowden's personality and my personality are just different on game day. I try to stay as calm

Georgia head coach Mark Richt, shown here during his days as Florida State's offensive coordinator, credits Bobby Bowden for providing a blueprint for life on and off the football field. *Courtesy of FSU Sports Information*

and peaceful as I can, and he gets excited. There is nothing wrong with that. It is just a different personality and a different style. He didn't get excited in a bad way. I get excited too, but I'm just not as verbal.

People will comment to me that I stay calm in the game, and that's a great thing. There are coaches who are more outwardly excited, and they can think straight and make great decisions that way.

NOW BRAD, BRAD, WHAT ARE WE DOING?

The experience under Coach Bowden was unbelievable. I'll never forget the gifts that I have been given—going back to my high school coach. Then in college, as a quarterback at Miami, I learned so much about football and the passing game from Coach Howard Schnellenberger, Earl Morrall, Gary Stevens, and Joe Brodsky. But to actually become a coach and to be able to start coaching under Bobby Bowden and to be at Florida State for the first 14 years of my coaching career, minus one at East Carolina, was just tremendous for me. I learned so much at East Carolina in just one year as a coordinator there in 1989. It was my first full-time job after being a graduate assistant and volunteer coach at Florida State, and I had to learn how to coach coaches and deal with the media. All of those opportunities really shaped me, but without a doubt, the most influential aspects of my coaching career and in my life are those that happened under Coach Bowden's influence.

There are a lot of stories that are funny now but weren't much fun then. For example, if we went one drive without scoring, maybe we wouldn't hear anything from Coach. But if we went two drives and didn't score, we were going to hear him piping up. The worse things got, the more he would speak up. When I was there as the coordinator after Brad Scott left following the 1994 Orange Bowl, he would start calling for me—"Mark, Mark, what is going on?"

Before you knew it, he would be calling for Brad. "Now Brad, Brad, what are we going to do?"

Then, if he really got jacked up, he would start calling for Wayne McDuffie, whose last year as coordinator at Florida State was 1989.

When it got to that point, I knew we were really in trouble and we had better score.

Something that happened a couple of times in my first year as coordinator involved Danny Kanell. He was the starting quarterback after Charlie Ward, and nobody could be as good as Charlie that first year. Danny was really a first-time starter and hadn't played much high school ball for that matter. We played Notre Dame in Orlando late that season, and I said, "Coach, we have to make a change here with Danny. He's struggling and is really killing us right now." And Coach said, "No, we aren't going to do it."

I would always defer to Coach because he was the boss. I think at times, he would look at that as a sign of weakness. He wanted somebody to battle him—to say, "No, dadgummit, this is what I believe." I'd say what I believed, and if he didn't want to do it, I would let him know that I respected my elders and respected my boss. He wished I would battle him more.

We kept Danny in that Notre Dame game, and he played good in the second half, and we ended up winning the game.

Then in the Florida game, we were losing 24–3 at halftime, and he was saying, "We have to make the change. We have to make the change."

I said, "Coach, I don't think he is the problem today. He's really playing pretty good, and I just don't think we are protecting him. We should keep him in there. I just think we should go to the no-huddle right out of the gate."

Thankfully, we came back to tie that thing, 31–31. That might have saved my coaching career right there. I don't know if I would have still been the coordinator after that day if we had been beat 51–3.

Like anybody, Coach liked calling the touchdown plays. The closer we got to the end zone, the more anxious he was to call one that would spin into the end zone. We opened the 1999 season against Louisiana Tech, and that was the game Peter Warrick had all those great moves on this one reverse. Coach Bowden had been anxious to call the reverse. We were up there trying to gauge whether the defensive ends were trying to squeeze the backside and doing the other things that need to happen for those reverses to come about. And we were telling Coach that it just didn't look like it was there for us. He finally got frustrated and called that son of a gun anyway. Of course, Peter dodged all those guys and scored, and then Coach said, "I told you, buddy. I told you it was there."

They were a lot of fun—the trick plays and, after a while, the kind of offense we ran.

The one we put in with Chris Weinke against Clemson in 2000, where we ran a play-action fake and then threw to "Snoop" Minnis from the back of the end zone for a 98-yard touchdown, was a play I learned from Coach Bowden. It was called against Auburn for Eric Thomas in the mid-1980s and was known as something like the Flatback Rooskie. I remember Coach taking the whole team into the minigym; we didn't practice that play outdoors. He showed everybody exactly how he wanted it done and how he wanted it acted out, and they did it. The play was so wide-open, it was unbelievable.

That made an impression on me. I used that play when I was at East Carolina to win a game we probably would have otherwise lost. At Florida State, we called it more than one time. When I came to Georgia, the first time we called it, it was a touchdown against Auburn. The next time we called it was a touchdown against Vandy, and the next time we ran it was a huge play that set up a touchdown in a game in which we had been stagnant against Georgia Tech.

Those are things that I saw Coach Bowden do, and the thing about Coach is he knew people were creatures of habit. He'd study that film, and every time he saw a pattern, he would try to exploit it. That's how that play from the end zone to Snoop worked. People didn't run that play, but close to the end zone they were running the ball out of a two-tight-end set with a little receiver motion to block a safety. We saw that every time that receiver went to block the safety, that Clemson corner would come up and support the run. The safety would try to dodge the block. We would say, "That's it—that's a Rooskie." We would talk about it in our "Iffy meeting" the night before the game— "Coach, I think the Rooskie is here, and this is why." I showed him the tape and said if we were on the 1-yard line that I thought we should call it.

His response was, "Go for it, buddy." So we did, and it worked.

That's something I definitely learned from him, and I still benefit from that thinking and approach. In our 2005 SEC championship game at Georgia, the first touchdown pass was a play we threw in the 1999 national championship game from Chris Weinke to Peter Warrick. We faked the slant and then went deep because of how we saw the defenders react. And I remembered that from what we did at Florida State.

The second touchdown pass we threw in the SEC championship game was another play we used at Florida State against Virginia that should have been a touchdown. We faked an audible like we were going to throw the quick pass, and then we saw how the defense would jump and then threw it deep. It was about doing things at the right time, and that's something that Coach Bowden did so well.

When you see the circumstances are right, you call those plays. I learned that from Coach Bowden—the art of looking for those opportunities. Under the right circumstances, that kind of play—a fake punt for example, which we ran in the 2005 season against Kentucky to get us in the SEC championship—could be 100 percent. It was that calculated risk. It was studied. It was planned, and we practiced it diligently. That was the secret to trick plays under Coach Bowden.

Coach Bowden always talked strategy and tactics. You could have great strategy, but if your tactics or execution of a play was poor, it would not work. He would always make the point that if you had average strategy with great tactics, you would succeed. But if you had great strategy without good execution, you would not have much success. So I learned that before you start slinging out those great trick plays, you better make sure the kids have confidence in them. That was just Coach Bowden's way.

THE RIVAL COACH

Bobby Bowden has frequently been asked to list the most memorable and meaningful of his 350-plus victories en route to attaining the most wins among NCAA Division I football coaches. Victories over Nebraska will always rank high among Bowden's favorites. In his first 30 years at Florida State University, Bowden defeated the Cornhuskers six times, and nearly each win had a significant impact on his football program.

In 1980, the Seminoles shocked the college football world with an 18–14 victory at then third-ranked Nebraska. Cornhuskers coach Tom Osborne will always remember that day for how hot it was and how hard FSU played. The victory helped establish Bobby Bowden as "King of the Road."

In the 1994 Orange Bowl against Nebraska, Bowden became king of college football. The Seminoles' 18–16 victory provided Bowden and the Seminoles a long-sought first national championship. In previous years, Bowden had bested Osborne in two Fiesta Bowls and in the 1993 Orange Bowl preceding their rematch for No. 1.

Osborne was a legendary coach who won three national titles and 12 bowl games. He later became a U.S. congressman.

From those high-stakes showdowns between Bowden and Osborne developed a mutual admiration that was as strong as the national power-houses they coached.

Bobby Bowden is someone I admire and respect. I've always believed that Bobby and I were on the same wavelength as far as caring about players, trying to play the right way, and opposing those things that aren't in the best interest of the game. Bobby has run his Florida State program in a solid, consistent way. I know his faith is very important, and he has promoted good values in his players. He treats his players and staff the right way. Those are qualities to admire in a coach. Bobby has definitely been good for the game of football.

It's pretty remarkable for someone to be coaching as long as he has and to be as successful as Coach Bowden has been throughout that span. It's not only a matter of being a very good coach, but it also reflects how Bobby looks at life—his outlook. If you are really, really intense and are driven and take yourself too seriously, I think it's hard to coach that long without coming to a point where you self-destruct.

But I know Bobby plays a little golf here and there. He has a good sense of humor, and he takes care of himself. That doesn't mean he isn't a competitor; he certainly is. But I just don't think you can go that long unless you have a pretty good philosophy regarding life. Of course, he is a very spiritual person, and I think that helps as well. He realizes there is something more important than the final score of a football game.

The average person will look at how many games Bobby has won and at his championships. What he accomplishes season after season is truly remarkable, as is his bowl record. At one time he won 11 consecutive bowl games. That degree of consistency is difficult to achieve. Some coaches can have certain things come together for one year, but somebody who does it year after year, as Bobby has, is somebody who has got it all together. I think winning all the games he has is certainly a sign of longevity, but it also speaks to him having coached so well. I think to have as many wins as he does is remarkable, but it is worth noting again that consistency. He had quite a streak.

But Bobby's real mark or legacy will be how his players have benefited from their relationship with him. In my experience, I believe that's probably the most satisfying and maybe the most important thing that any coach can achieve over time—to leave a legacy of improving the lives of most people you touch. Certainly, you don't win every battle.

Legendary Nebraska coach Tom Osborne (L) found Bobby Bowden's team to be well prepared and tough to beat. *Courtesy of FSU Sports Information*

Bobby honestly cares about his players, and Kevin Steele, who was with me at Nebraska and is now a coach at Florida State, tells me that it is something that still stands out about Bobby. He is not going to throw players away just because they made a mistake. And I think that's an admirable quality—that he supports his players as best he can.

Bobby and I were very similar in our approach in the way we handled our players. You want to be like a parent to them, and I think Bobby has tried to be that. Some people want to just dismiss a player. But my philosophy, and I think it's one we shared, is you don't want to take them away from the support that they have in college with coaches and teachers. I think it's proven that the future doesn't bode well for them if you do.

Bobby's teams were always hard to prepare for simply because they executed so well. They had great athletes who were well prepared and motivated; we did the best we could. Bobby always had a trick play for us, and of course, he is known for that. But the main thing was stopping Florida State's base stuff—the plays that we knew they were going to run. Sometimes they had such good players that they were just going to run them anyway, and they would be successful at it. That was the most difficult thing in preparing for Bobby's teams—the players he had. That was especially true in those later meetings that took place between us. We were having to defend against Charlie Ward and players such as him who were just great athletes.

Bobby always had a very balanced offence, whereas at Nebraska we tended to run the ball more than we threw it. But Bobby tended to run it and throw it fairly equally. That always made it harder to prepare for a team like his if you don't know whether they are going to run and throw.

Bobby's Florida State teams are always well-coached. They always put a lot of emphasis on the kicking game. There wasn't going to be any phase that he wasn't well-prepared. That was just something you knew to expect from a Bobby Bowden–coached team.

THE FIRST MEETING

When Bobby went to Florida State, they were certainly in tough shape financially, and they were having to play a lot of really good teams on the road. It was a tough deal for any team to have to do that. But Bobby began to win a fair number of those games, and I think that's where he showed his real merit as a coach.

We weren't surprised by the kind of team he had the first time he came to Nebraska to play us in 1980. We had seen what he had done at West Virginia and what he was trying to accomplish at Florida State. He was just a very sound coach and did a great job with that team.

I had that sense for Bobby and his program that first time he came to Nebraska and played. The temperature on the field was between 115 and 120, and near the end of the game, both teams were pretty tired yet were playing very hard. I'm sure I had seen him at some convention or someplace else before that day, but when we talked after that game and then again later, our friendship started to develop.

Bobby was a very good friend, and it wasn't unusual for us to talk about how we approached different aspects of the game. That may have hurt our program to some degree. I really admired his bowl record, and I went down to Tallahassee one time to talk with him about how well he was doing in the bowl games. I found out he prepared differently than we did for the bowls. For us, when the regular season was over, we might take two or three days off, but then we would practice for the bowl game three or four times a week. We would never take much of a break, but I found that Bobby's team was taking a couple of weeks off after the regular season. For him and the passing game, that break was a good thing. But in our case, with option football, timing was so critical that when we started doing what Bobby had been doing, we had four or five years when we didn't do as well in the bowl games. Execution in the option game really required us to stick with our heavy practice schedule. So out of that friendship resulted a bad decision, but I don't blame Bobby. He found the fit that worked for him. The proof is in his record.

We freely traded information and film, and I believe that was mostly beneficial, and that reflected on our relationship. We had a great relationship. I went down and visited with him in Tallahassee, and he had coaches come up to Nebraska in the spring. We traded a lot of ideas. That included not just Xs and Os, but also how we attempted to run our programs in the off-season. Both of us put a great emphasis on the off-season work of our players.

In the 1994 Orange Bowl, they may have had as good an offensive football team with Charlie Ward that I can remember ever coaching against. That game was a roller coaster of emotions. They came down to kick that field goal toward the end, and before that, there was a fourth-down play right near midfield that resulted in a measurement. It was about an inch; Florida State had made it. Had they not, the game would have been over. Then they made a couple of passes, got a penalty on us, and kicked a field goal to go ahead.

There were 21 seconds left, and we got a couple of passes and lined up for a 45-yard field goal. Bobby, from his sideline, thought the game was over and that he had won. The players even doused him with water. The official came over and said to him, "There's another second left."

We tried the field goal, and it certainly was in reasonable range, but we missed it. It was a tough game to lose.

But if I have to lose to somebody, I'd just as soon lose to Bobby.

BILLY SMITH

---◦═══◦○◦═══◦---

THE CONFIDANT

Billy Smith has been protecting Florida State head coaches since 1964. Smith was still a member of the Florida Highway Patrol when he stood between Coach Bill Peterson and any potential trouble at games on the road and at home. Smith, who retired as a major in 1985, has missed just six games in his role as head of security for FSU head football coaches. Prostate cancer kept him from games as did an earlier surgery; the marriage of his daughter, Terri; and a death in the family.

One absence came in 2003 when FSU played host to Colorado. Smith was ill, and director of sports medicine Randy Oravetz had to tell Bobby Bowden that Smith would not be at his side during the game. This news came at a point in the season when Bobby's son Jeff Bowden was already facing criticism as FSU's offensive coordinator. Oravetz asked Bobby Bowden if he needed another state trooper near him during the game.

Bowden answered, "No. I think I'll be OK. But you might want to get one for Jeff."

Wit is just one of the many qualities that Smith has come to admire in the Florida State head coach. With all the time that Smith spends with Bowden on football weekends, his role has expanded from that of protector to confidant.

My role, dealing with crowd issues and keeping watch on Coach Bowden, has always been challenging enough. But there was one time when I became extremely concerned for his safety more than any other. It was November 3, 1990, when Florida State played up at South Carolina, and it happened before the game was even played.

Coach Bowden's secretary, Sue Hall, called me earlier that week and said, "You need to come to the office immediately." I knew it had to be something serious by the tone in her voice. So I left my house and drove over to Florida State and went into the football coaches' offices.

She handed me a letter and said, "You need to read this." Now, keep in mind, all correspondence for Coach Bowden was opened by Sue Hall. If it was a bad letter, she'd throw it in the trash can. If it were something nice, she would pass it on.

This letter was postmarked from Pittsburgh. In the letter, this guy writes a hateful message to Coach Bowden and ends it with, "I'm going to kill you during the next out-of-town ball game." The week before, I guess, this guy had bet quite a bit of money on Florida State, and the Seminoles hadn't covered whatever the point spread was. So he was mad enough to write a letter saying he was going to kill Coach Bowden.

I met with Coach Bowden and the athletic director at the time, Hootie Ingram, and I said, "I don't want you to tell anybody about this. No one, and I mean no one, needs to know about this."

Coach Bowden asked me, "What are you going to do?"

I said, "I don't have any idea, but let me tell you something up-front. The president of the United States has got the best security in the world, and even the president is shot once in a while. I'm going to do my best to make sure that doesn't happen to you."

My suggestion to him was, "Coach the game and let me take care of the other part of it. And just maybe, we can come through it OK."

I got 20 guys with the South Carolina law enforcement agency, which would be that state's version of the Florida Department of Law Enforcement. I had 20 guys from their agency in plain clothes working the game. They were on the sideline with us. I knew there were a lot of extra police at the ball game, but I didn't really know how many until after the game.

During the ball game, several of our coaches came up to me yelling, "Billy, your buddies here, they're getting in our way," meaning the police officers.

I told them, "I understand, but they're doing their job, and they're doing it well." They didn't have any idea what was going on. But when you add 20 officers who normally are not on the sideline, it's hard for them not to get in the way.

So anyway, the game ended, and Florida State won big, 41–10. Everybody on our side was happy. We came off the field, and I had told Coach Bowden that we would go right off the field, no delaying.

I had told Coach Bowden before he came out of that dressing room that I was going to back the trooper car up as close to this door as I could possibly get it.

"When we walk out of this door, we're moving," I said. "We're not going to take pictures; we're not going to shake hands; we're not going to talk to anybody. We're going—fast."

We jumped into that trooper car, and we left the buses and took off and went to the airport. Fortunately, nothing happened. We got back safely, and there was never another threat on his life.

The Monday after the game, Coach Bowden called me and said, "I know what you told me about the threat, and it just didn't ring a bell with me. But when I walked out of that locker-room door, my heart dropped to pure bottom."

Yes, I was concerned. That's why I arranged for so much security and had a plan to get him out of that stadium. As I told Coach Bowden, if somebody wants to shoot you, they can shoot you—maybe at your house, maybe at the grocery store, maybe getting out of your car. But if they really want to shoot you, they can. We can do some things that can reduce that or try to prevent it, but if they want to shoot you, they can.

In that particular instance, we were lucky, and we never heard any more about it.

Ann Bowden may have known about the death threat, but if she did, she didn't express it. The players didn't know. The coaches didn't know. Fortunately, that was the only time something like that happened.

BOWDEN FAMILY TRAGEDY

The threat on Coach Bowden's life was the most difficult game situation, but it wasn't the toughest thing I've ever done. The most dif-

Whether it was a pregame entrance, or postgame meeting with an opposing coach, Billy Smith ensured Bobby Bowden had a secure route.
Courtesy of Ryals Lee, FSU Photo Lab

ficult time for me was the night Coach Bowden lost his grandson and his former son-in-law in a car accident.

It happened on a Sunday night, September 5, 2004, after the Florida State–Miami game had been rescheduled for that following Friday due to a hurricane threat. I received a call that night from the Florida Highway Patrol about a bad wreck in Gadsden County, which is the county just west of Leon County and Tallahassee.

The officers told me that it was a fatal wreck and they thought some of Coach Bowden's relatives were involved. One of the people didn't have any identification, but the police ran a check on the car tag. So I left my house and went out to meet the officers. It was confirmed that John Madden, who was married to Coach Bowden's youngest daughter, Ginger, along with their son, Bowden Madden, who was a high school football player in Fort Walton Beach, had died in the crash.

Then I had to go back and tell Coach Bowden and his family.

When I got up to their house that night, it was about ten o'clock. Coach Bowden usually goes to bed about seven o'clock when he's not involved in football games. I rang the doorbell. Ginger answered the door, and I was thinking, "Lord, have mercy. How do I handle this?"

All I could say is, "Ginger, we need to sit down. I've got some bad, bad news for you." Before I could get the words out, she lost it. Ann Bowden was lying on the sofa asleep. She immediately woke up. Then I had to go through that with her. Coach Bowden was upstairs sleeping. He heard the screams and came down the stairs. Then I had to tell him.

By this time, two of the highway patrol officers who had worked the wreck knocked on the door. Coach Bowden, being the detail person he is, wanted a diagram of how that wreck happened. I think that was so he could rationalize it in his own mind, so the officers diagrammed it for him.

He said, "OK," and that was it.

He said to me, "I've never, ever handled a funeral before. I need your help." So I did what I could, advising him to call a funeral home, set up a preacher, things like that. It was getting to be near midnight when I said to Coach Bowden, "You need to call all the immediate family, all of your sons, and tell them. Don't let them hear this from the media or someone else."

He called Terry, Tommy, and Jeff. He got everybody except Steve, and he left a message with him.

Bowden Madden was a very special grandson. He was a football player. I can't even convey how difficult this was. And then, Coach Bowden and the family had to go to a funeral for his grandson and former son-in-law, then fly to Miami and play a football game against the Miami Hurricanes.

I know how it ate him alive. It tore me up. That night at his house was the longest night of my life. It seemed 40 hours long.

In my line of work as a highway patrol officer, I've had to go to a lot of houses and inform family of a fatal car accident, but this was so different. Oh boy, was it ever different because this was my buddy, Coach Bowden, sitting there, and I had to tell him. And he was hurting big-time. It just eats you alive. I don't care what you try to say, the right words don't come out.

FORGING A RELATIONSHIP

I first met Coach Bowden when he was an assistant at Florida State in 1964. At the time, I was working security for Coach Bill Peterson since he was the man in charge. My conversations with Coach Bowden were nothing more than "Hey, how are you doing? I'm Bobby Bowden," that type of thing. And that's the way it stayed the entire year.

We went to the Gator Bowl that year and beat Oklahoma. Shortly thereafter, Coach Bowden left to become an assistant coach at West Virginia before getting the head coaching job. I stayed on at Florida State, working security under the other head coaches who followed Coach Pete: Larry Jones and Darrell Mudra.

In 1976, when Coach Bowden was hired as the new Florida State coach, we met again. He remembered me, but things were totally different because I was going to be working as his security officer. We met at a Holiday Inn in Tallahassee and had a long talk after he was announced for the job. His message to me was, "Just look after me. If you see I'm doing something I might not need to do, or if there is anything I need to do, let me know."

Back then, keep in mind, he wasn't what you would call a hot commodity—a person whose autograph everybody would want. That wasn't it at all.

In his first year, we weren't very good. We went 5-6 that season. In the second game, we played at Miami. Boy, they were killing us. They wound up beating us 47–0 that day. During the game, Coach Bowden paced up and down the sideline. I couldn't resist. I said, "Coach, I think I know how to put an end to this thing."

He said, "What do you mean?"

I said, "Tell our nose guard to throw the ball up in the stands and make the referee go hunt it every time he lays it down."

He told me later on, "I should have taken your advice."

Another funny story happened a few years later. We were out in the western part of the country playing in a game. I can't remember if it was Arizona State or San Diego State, but it was a school out west. Anyway, after the game, Coach Bowden and I were standing outside a state trooper's car waiting for everybody to get dressed and loaded up.

An elderly lady walked across the parking lot, yelling, "Young man, young man," and I said, "Coach, I know she wants me, because I'm younger than you are." So I went over to meet her. I said, "Ma'am, if you need directions, I can't help you. I'm not from here. But I'll be happy to find some directions."

She said, "Oh no, I live here. I graduated from Florida State in 1939. I moved out here to become a teacher, and I retired as a teacher."

She told me, "When I have the girls over"—and she meant other retired teachers—"I see the Florida State team on television. They change colors. Sometimes they have dark colors, and other times they wear white colors. But when I see you in that uniform, I know that's my team.

"I do have one complaint, if you don't mind."

I said, "Well, I think you're entitled to a complaint."

She said, "Every time I see you on television, there's a little short man standing in front of you, sometimes wearing something on his head.

"You know, it's so rude. You would really think he would get out of the way. He's not a young man, either. Surely, his mother taught him better.

"Now, I don't mean to hurt his feelings; he just needs to move out of the way."

Well, it was all I could do to keep from laughing, knowing she was talking about Coach Bowden being that little, short man. So I immediately conveyed that to Coach Bowden, about how he was always in my way on the sideline.

A couple of games later, we were playing in Tallahassee, and right during the game he said, "I'm not getting in your way, am I?"

I said, "You're doing OK."

Obviously, he doesn't have a script laid out for this stuff. It's just off-the-cuff, whatever it may be. But he is a very funny man. Some things he says he may not intend to be funny but just come out that way—low-key, easygoing, humorous.

One example happened against Nebraska one season. Brad Scott was a coach and was in charge of various other things during the game.

During the game, I bet you Coach Bowden asked Brad about 100 times about a time-clock issue: "Are you sure you are correct?"

Brad kept saying, "Oh yes sir, yes sir."

Coach Bowden said to him, "Well, you better be, because if you're not, I'm going to take Billy's gun and shoot you!"

He said this right in middle of the game.

Brad kept mumbling something, saying, "Coach, I got it covered."

I guess I've dealt with all sorts of crowd situations. One of the most memorable was in 1977 after Florida State beat Florida for the first time in 10 years. We drove back, and it was a really big deal to beat Florida back then. So as our caravan turned off Interstate 10 onto Mahan Drive, outside of Tallahassee, there were cars parked everywhere. I'm talking about hundreds of cars and people lining this entire route. They were standing on the side of the road, waving and yelling in support.

We got near the stadium, and there was no plan—nothing. We just pulled into the stadium lot, and there were thousands of people there. There were no lights on, nothing but a sea of people.

As we got out of the patrol car, Ann Bowden was holding onto my belt. Coach Bowden was right by my side. We went straight out into the middle of the football field. Pretty soon, everybody in the traveling party with the team was on the field. There were no speakers and no lights, but we walked all the way across the field. Don't ask me why we did it that way, but I thought it was the only way we could get out of there without being mobbed.

You know how people have a tendency to do some drinking? There were some folks who were really celebrating that night. Everybody wanted to hug Coach Bowden's neck and shake his hand. And the only thing I told him was, "Let's keep moving."

We didn't know where we were going. We just hit the football field. I didn't know what we were going to do, truthfully, but I just knew that, well, I knew where the football training center was, so I said, "Let's head that way."

Another time the crowd was a big issue was after we lost to Virginia on their field in 1995. That was a big-time concern. The second the game ended, I grabbed Coach Bowden by the arm and people poured on that field.

I said, "Coach, we're not going anywhere."

He said, "I got to see George," meaning George Welsh, who was the Virginia head coach at the time.

He kept saying, "I got to see George."

I said, "We're not going anywhere. People will mob us out there."

Of course by then, all these kids, Virginia students, were on the field, knocking and banging us as they ran by to get to midfield. So we went off in a different direction to the field house.

Coach Bowden called George on Monday and apologized for not congratulating him on the field.

George told him, "That was the first time I ever feared for my life on a football field. If I could have run, I would have been gone too." In that situation, you never know what young kids, half-drunk, are going to do.

That was the only time Coach Bowden didn't meet the opposing coach after the game.

TOUGH LOSSES, QUIET TIMES

The game I saw him hurt the most is when we played Auburn up there in 1983. For Coach Bowden, a game against Auburn was like going back home. It was family and friends; it was home to him.

Well, Florida State lost the game 27–24, right at the end. Bo Jackson was playing for Auburn at the time, and he just took over the game.

Afterward, in the locker room, there wasn't a nice meeting with the players. It got a little personal. Coach Bowden finished, and just before we got ready to leave the locker room, he asked me, "Who's riding with you?"

I figured he wanted somebody else in the car with us, so I said, "Coach, it's just you and me and—" then he stopped me.

He said, "I don't want anybody else in the car."

He got in the car and said, "I don't want the radio on. I don't want any talking. I just want quiet time."

I said, "Coach, we've got about three hours together until we get to Tallahassee. I hear what you're saying. Trust me; the radio won't be turned on. I'll turn the police radio off.

"If at any time, between here and there, you decide you want a cold drink or you want to talk or whatever, you let me know. Otherwise, we've got three hours of silence."

As we pulled out of that gate, he started talking. And he never stopped talking.

We stopped at a convenience store; he got an orange drink with peanuts. When he got back in the car, he started talking again, and we discussed that game the entire way back to Tallahassee. It was three hours of me listening to him talk about what could have been. That loss just tore at him.

A much funnier experience with Coach Bowden and me in the patrol car happened after we won at Florida in 2003. That was the game where we pulled it out in the last minute.

A writer from *ESPN The Magazine*, Gene Wojciechowski, wanted to ride back with us so he could get some exclusive thoughts from Coach Bowden about the game. He said he had cleared it with Coach Bowden, and I said, "That's good, and I'm sure you have, but before we do this, I'll talk to him." Coach Bowden said it was perfectly OK, so the three of us got in the car and headed out.

Now, keep in mind, Coach Bowden does this unique thing after a game. It's called "going to sleep." Believe me, this wasn't a two- or three-hour interview. Gene wound up talking to me because there was no one else to talk to. Coach Bowden was asleep most of the time. He was awake for about 15 minutes coming out of Gainesville and about 15 to 20 minutes until we got to Tallahassee, but that's how he is. He's able to go to sleep. When we're together in the car after the game, we very seldom talk about football. We talk about family, relationships, the important things in life. It's more like, "How is old so-and-so doing?"

When we're riding before a game, I don't ever say a word to him. For example, when we're playing at Florida and we're staying at Lake City—that's about a 45-minute drive from Gainesville—I don't say a word to him.

It's not one of these conversations like, "Are we going to get them?" Coach Bowden is very quiet. Outwardly, he never gets too high.

I guess the highest compliment he's ever paid me happened a few years ago. The team always stays in Thomasville, Georgia, on the nights before home games. The team trainer, Randy Oravetz, came up to me Saturday morning before we left for Tallahassee and said, "You need to buy about 50 newspapers."

I said, "For what?"

Well, come to find out, the *Tallahassee Democrat* had done a story on Coach Bowden, a profile on him and some of his personal thoughts. In the story, Coach Bowden said the three people he admired the most were his father, who was dead; Billy Graham; and Billy Smith.

So Monday morning I called and said, "I need to see Coach Bowden."

I went into his office and said, "Let's talk." I said, "That's probably the highest compliment anybody has ever paid me."

He said, "Well, I meant every word of it."

Coach Bowden doesn't have a lot of what you might call close friends. He has a lot of acquaintances and such, but not a lot of real close friends.

He told me, "Well, you know, during football season I spend more time with you than I do with Ann. And there are some things from time to time that I don't need to talk to Ann about, but I need to talk to somebody about, and you're a good sounding board for me. The other thing I appreciate is you're very honest with me, but I never hear it repeated again, and that's important to me."

I didn't wind up buying 50 newspapers. I got two or three, but I still say, without a doubt, that it was quite an honor.

TOUGH TO SAY NO

In 1993, Florida State played at Maryland. Somebody convinced Coach Bowden he needed to sign a couple footballs there for some underprivileged children. On Friday night before the game, we went to Cole Field House, the old basketball arena for Maryland, and we walked up seven flights of stairs to where this guy was set up with a table. We got up there, and the guy had arranged about 200 footballs to sign. Quarterback Charlie Ward was there with us.

I said to Coach Bowden, "You make the call. If you want to do it, I'll set up a little system. I don't want you standing up all night, signing footballs."

He said, "Yeah, I'd like to do it."

So I set it up with Coach and Charlie sitting two seats apart, and I got some other volunteers, and we got those footballs passed in a line until they signed each one.

As we were leaving, Coach Bowden said to me, "We're not going to let that happen again, are we?"

I said, "No, sir, we're not."

Well, to make it even worse, I found out the next day that, of all those footballs signed, only two of the footballs went to underprivileged kids. The rest were sold to boosters.

I got hold of someone from the Maryland athletic department and said, "Don't you ever, ever, ask Coach Bowden to come back again. All you had to do was be honest. Don't play games with us."

But Coach Bowden is usually more than willing to sign autographs. It doesn't matter who it is or what type of clothes the person has on.

After we played at Notre Dame up in 2003—it was a big win, 37–0—Coach Bowden was all dressed and ready to leave the locker room when he asked me, "Are you game for something?"

He said, "Why don't we go out and sign some autographs?"

We went out of Notre Dame Stadium, and this was probably an hour after the game. There were probably 300 people, all Notre Dame folks, milling around. Coach Bowden signed every autograph, had pictures made, whatever everybody wanted.

He always liked Notre Dame. When he was following Alabama during the 1950s, back then, Notre Dame was it. There was no such thing as television. But on radio, it was Notre Dame. They were the big dogs: them, Oklahoma, Southern Cal—those teams. So he has a lot of respect for Notre Dame.

I don't think many people really understand what Coach Bowden's done for Florida State on a national level. Sure, he's had a bump or two with some of his players getting in trouble. But I venture to say you could take any 100 people who graduate from high school and go to college and watch all those people and see what happens to them. How many wind up in jail? How many wind up to be doctors or successful? Coach Bowden has to be a father figure to about 100 kids, 100 young men, every year.

STUCK IN THE BIG EASY

Coach Bowden is probably the most time-conscious guy I've ever known in my life. I mean, being off five minutes here or there makes him uncomfortable. He likes a routine.

With that in mind, imagine how upset he was on a September Friday in 1983 when we traveled to play Tulane in New Orleans. Before we arrived, I had called the state police, and they assured me they were going to have motorcycles and cars waiting to escort us downtown.

We arrived at the airport in New Orleans, and there were no cars, no motorcycles, or anything. Coach Bowden immediately wanted to know what had happened to the transportation.

I got on the phone and called the Louisiana state police, and a dispatcher said to me, "Well, they're escorting your team right now."

I said, "Oh yeah? Well, not really."

Then I found out the police were escorting the University of Central Florida football team, which was playing Southeastern Louisiana the next day, but staying in New Orleans. Their plane had come in five minutes ahead of us.

The UCF athletic director is Bill Peterson, who used to be the Florida State head coach. So, of course, when a police officer greeted him at the airport and said, "Are you the team from Florida?" Peterson said "Oh, absolutely."

By then, we couldn't get anybody else to escort us. And it was five o'clock on a Friday afternoon in New Orleans. The traffic was thick as could be. If that wasn't bad enough, we got out on the interstate, and there was a semitrailer turned over on the highway. The traffic was backed up.

When we got to the hotel, the New Orleans Marriott, it turned out that UCF was also staying there too. The hotel was besieged, and our rooms weren't ready. The players had to meet out in the hallway. Then we played Tulane the next day and got beat 38–34. That was the game where Tulane was later ruled to have used an ineligible player and it became a forfeit win. But Coach Bowden was fit to be tied. After everything that had happened, then to lose the game, he was real mad.

While in the locker room, the Tulane coach, Wally English, popped his head in and said he wanted to meet Coach Bowden to congratulate him on a good game.

I told him, "It would have been a good game if we had won like we were supposed to have won." I said to the coach, "Now is not a good time to meet Coach Bowden."

Well, I got distracted, and lo and behold, Wally English had gotten into the locker room, and he and Coach Bowden were engaged in conversation as if nothing had happened.

A FATHER FIGURE, A BEST FRIEND

My father and I were never real close when I was growing up. After I got out of high school, I went into the Air Force and did things away from home. So I never really had a father figure most of my life.

But Coach Bowden is not only like a father figure to me, he's my friend. He's always there for me. He's always accessible. If I've ever needed to talk to him, he's always been available for me.

So for Billy Smith, he's been quite an inspiration.

He's never lied to me. He's never done anything that would tarnish his image. And just to see what he has done for this university, it's amazing. It's amazing when you travel outside the state and you have a Florida State shirt on or something else, how many people might recognize it and say they are fans of Coach Bowden.

There's a word in the dictionary called *integrity*. To me, it's one of the most important words in the dictionary. And I think Coach Bowden is the definition of integrity.

One of the things Coach Bowden and I have never, ever talked about is a thing called retirement. Instead, we've talked about things like "when this is all over"—that type of thing. But as far as setting up a day and planning for a retirement, I don't think he knows when he'll do that. As long as his health is good, he's winning, and he's enjoying doing what he's doing, he'll be here. He'll set the time; nobody else will.

THE SECRETARY

To the players, from Deion Sanders to Charlie Ward to Derrick Brooks to Chris Weinke, she was known simply as "Miss Sue." Sue Hall had a short title for such a demanding, multifaceted role in Florida State's football operations. She was more than Bobby Bowden's secretary from 1979 through 2000. She was a guidance counselor, a den mother, and an adviser on boyfriend-girlfriend relationships. As a notary, she married friends and strangers. She handled the Mount Everest of memorabilia that piled in her office. She dealt with daily media requests. She calmed the emotions of coaches. But most of all, she tirelessly worked to ensure Bowden had the smoothest days possible. Her loyalty to Bowden was matched by her passion to handle a job requiring seven-day workweeks, varied hours, and daily pressure. She played switchboard operator, game plan coordinator, and birthday-party planner. But no matter whether it was Burt Reynolds in her office or a fan seeking a picture, Miss Sue remained unfazed and never frazzled.

During the years I worked for Coach Bowden, people were always very curious of my job. Some people, I guess, were in awe. That used to crack me up. I would have people come up to me and ask, "Oh, what's it like to work for Bobby Bowden? You must have the best job in the world."

And I would tell them, "You wouldn't want it."

They would ask me if it was a lot of fun, and I would say, "No, it's not fun." You might think it would be, but it's not. He's a taskmaster.

It's hard work. It's very hard. You have to be a certain type of person to last.

He was a very tough boss. People thought because Coach Bowden was so friendly he would be easy to work for. Well, he's nothing like he is in public, because in the office he's working. Think about it. Football is a multimillion-dollar business. The CEO has to be tough.

I would tell people we worked hard. We started off our days working, and we didn't stop. Just like he did to the assistant coaches, Coach Bowden would give me a task and he would expect it to be done correctly. But the volume of work never bothered me. Before I got the job in 1979, I had worked for a lawyer for 17 years. That helped prepare me because in that job, everything was "Do it right now. Get it done correctly." So I was used to working under stress from that.

But I really didn't know about stress. I just took on a job and did it. I was a workaholic. I came in early and worked long hours, and that never bothered me. But if I was not married to who I was married to, a husband who loved football; and if my children had not already been grown, I would not have been able to do the job.

When I interviewed for the job, I knew nothing about Coach Bowden. Absolutely nothing. I had been going to FSU football games since I was probably 18 or 19 years old. I remember some of the former head coaches, Larry Jones and Bill Peterson, and all that, but other than the name, I knew nothing about Coach Bowden.

I think he had two or three secretaries before me. And the reason none of them lasted might have been their age. When I came to the interview, he said, "I'm looking for a mama for these kids, because I'm their daddy." Well, I had raised three boys, so I imagined I could fill that bill, and that's the way I got the job.

The interview went real well. He didn't say much; I did most of the talking. Because I really wanted the job, I just told him the truth: "Hey, my husband coaches youth football. I'm the biggest cheerleader. I've been going out to FSU games all these years. I'm a big football fan—season-ticket holder"—all that. I wanted to let him know I had a background even though I knew nothing about football other than what I had learned by watching my husband coach.

He said, "I don't want any single women, and I don't want any divorced women, because I've got coaches who are here that don't see their wives and who spend long hours here." I appreciated that in him. We didn't hire secretaries who were divorced. No temptations there—if that's a good way to put it. I thought that was very good of him to look after his staff that way.

You would not believe the facilities back then. They were nothing like they are now. When I first started, there was just a little building for the coaches' offices underneath the football stands. The women and the men who worked in the office shared the same bathroom. If it was raining or cold, we had to go through the football locker room to go to the dining area. I had to yell to announce that a woman was walking through.

THE AURA OF BOWDEN

He was meticulous, but so was I. Every day, I cleaned his desk and dusted. He liked the things in his drawer a certain way. He was very organized, and if I dusted the desk and moved something over, then he moved it back. He was very neat in what he did. Even books on the shelf were a certain way.

He treated me the same way he treated his coaches. He expected me to do everything with very little supervision. And when people do that, I think you work harder to please them. I worked very hard to make sure everything was right, to make sure everybody was working and the office was run well.

I don't know why, but I never got caught up in the fact I was working for somebody famous. It was just like my relationship with Burt Reynolds. He's just a person to me.

I would always get amused at how other people reacted around Coach Bowden. One day, a lady and her husband came in to get something autographed. I knew this woman pretty well. Coach Bowden happened to be in the office. It was during the summer, and we weren't real busy, so I asked him if it was OK to bring them into his office.

Well, after I introduced them, she just sat there and looked at him. He talked to her for a few minutes, and when it was time to go, her

In her 22 years as Bobby Bowden's secretary, Sue Hall had many memorable moments, such as this opportunity with Bobby Bowden and the crystal national championship trophy following the Seminoles' undefeated season in 1999. *Courtesy of FSU Sports Information*

husband said, "C'mon, let's go." But she just sat there, looking at Coach Bowden. I finally went over and pulled her arm to get her out of the chair. It's so funny how people reacted.

My own granddaughter was probably five years old when I introduced her to him. She never said a word, she just looked at him. And after he went back into the office, she said, "Bobby Bowden. Bobby Bowden. Bobby Bowden." I didn't realize his impact until I watched other people's reactions.

The public has no idea how many people want a piece of him all the time. They don't have a clue. The number of requests we received every year was absolutely overwhelming.

One time a writer, Ben Brown, was doing a book during the 1991 season on the team and Coach Bowden. He asked me, "How many requests does Coach Bowden get every day? How many things does he sign?" We had a gentleman in town, Chuck Tanner, who had volunteered to help me to answer these questions. I said, "OK, Chuck, we're going to chronicle and keep track of everything that comes into this office from August to December." When we finished, there were a little over 5,000 different items, and Coach Bowden had signed them all.

Of course, that did not include what was brought to his home, what he signed at fan day, and what he may have signed while bumping into someone on the street. That's just what came into our office.

TAKING CARE OF HIS PLAYERS

Coach Bowden had an open-door policy. His door was always open to his players. No matter who else was in that office, if a player came in and wanted him, he was available to him. In the early days, when Coach Bowden wasn't pulled from pillar to post, he took a lot of time with players, and they would go in and out of his office a lot.

You take William Floyd. He came by every single day. He and Coach Bowden had conversations. Sometimes they just sat and looked at each other. William was good about coming in every day, because he knew he had to. Coach Bowden told him to come in, and he was there. That's something I respect in a player—a feeling from him that says, "I know this coach is trying to help me, and so I will be there." I have no idea what they talked about, but I know William Floyd turned out to be a pretty good guy.

Todd Williams was another guy. I feel like Coach Bowden saved him also. That young man had really had a tough life, and for him just to be able to relate his story to Coach Bowden and for Coach Bowden to understand and know how to work with him may have made a difference. That's when you appreciate what Coach Bowden does for his players—the interest he takes in them as a person as well as an athlete. That's some of the respect I see in him and that I feel for him.

There were a lot of things that happened with players that I can't mention, but looking back, those were some things I can laugh about now—especially the times he had to go up to Burt Reynolds Hall to take care of a problem. He used to get calls from the dorm manager, and off he would go. I mean, he would drop what he was doing, and he'd be out the door and headed straight up there. It would happen a couple of times a season.

As we kept winning games and the program got bigger and bigger, the players had so much to deal with. Charlie Ward, for example, would get so much mail. One woman wrote him from Panama City, saying she wanted to be his girlfriend and wanted to marry him. Total stranger. All kinds of stuff came in for Charlie.

Coach Bowden would come in and share these things with me. We would try to help the players deal with all the mail and all the things being thrown at them.

Warrick Dunn, when he played here, once came into my office and told me, "Miss Sue, you cannot imagine the temptations that are out there for us. You cannot believe what we have to turn our backs on." He was very serious about that, and I knew. I could see it every day. The players had a lot to deal with.

A TYPICAL DAY DURING FOOTBALL SEASON

The first thing he would do every morning is meet with his coaches for devotion. That would start every day at eight o'clock. I would be in the office by seven. Sometimes I would get there at six.

I had to go in every day and get his day ready for him so that everything would be on his desk. I used to have these legal cards I would type up to let him know what he was doing all day long. That's what he went by. If it wasn't on that card, then it wasn't supposed to happen.

But every day began with a devotion. Each coach had to do a devotion. And when the graduate assistant coaches would first come there, they would be real nervous because they were required to do a devotion too. It went around the table with the coaches, so I used to keep a little devotion book or an inspiration book for them.

They would come in scared to death, telling me, "This is my first time." I would tell them, "That is the reason I keep these books." The devotion would last 30 minutes, then they would get down to business.

All of the staff would be in that office. Randy Oravetz, our head athletic trainer, would be in there, going over who was sick, hurt, whatever—all that. The strength coach would go over his little bit, then the recruiting coordinator, and so forth. And we had better be on time. The phones usually started ringing before eight o'clock in the morning. I did not believe in having an answering machine pick up the phone calls. I felt like a person should answer those phones and be available.

There were a lot of requests for letters. The requests were amazing. A wife would call and say, "My husband is dying. Can Coach Bowden send a letter?" And he would always send a picture and put something on it, usually a Bible verse. We would get wonderful feedback on that. We would have people call and say, "My husband was in the hospital, and when he got the picture, it was the first time I'd seen him smile in weeks. So when we buried him, the picture went into his coffin with him."

You don't know what kind of impact somebody like Coach Bowden plays in a person's life until you watch it day after day. And he did have a big impact on people.

We would get letters, for example, from parents whose kids were getting ready for their Bar Mitzvahs, and so I talked to Jewish friends of mine and learned how to write a letter and say the right words in order to help Coach Bowden out. You cannot believe the praise we got back.

We would get so many letters from mothers who would say, "My son is not doing well in school," or "I can't reach him anymore," and we would think, "Why do people think Coach Bowden can help their sons?" But he did. He would write them, and he always wrote, "God first, family second, then school." And he would always say something like, "Go to church. Read your Bible. Study hard. And mind your mom and dad." He said normal, everyday things.

We used to buy a lot of wedding cards, and he would sign the cards and send the cards to couples, and that would just thrill 'em to death—especially the people who said they were Seminoles and had always loved FSU.

A lot of Boy Scouts who became Eagle Scouts would ask Coach Bowden if he could be there at the ceremony. We'd send a note of con-gratulations. Those requests would often come from fathers.

A lot of people would name their pet dogs Bowden. We used to get pictures with a Seminoles scarf around the dog—a lot of those. There were just so many things that you cannot believe some of the stuff he signed. There were dog leashes; baby shoes; and old, scroungy hats that I wouldn't even want to touch, but which were somebody's good luck hats, and they were proud of them. So he signed them. He would always take the time.

What was interesting was to watch him actually sign his name, to watch how he signed an autograph. He would sign it very clearly, legibly. He used to tell his players, "Don't scratch your name. Sign it so people can read it." He felt at some point our names might be all we have, so be proud of them. I always thought that was interesting. "Be proud of your name and write it so people can see it."

During our annual fan-photo day in August, right before the season, people would get in this long line around the building to get Coach Bowden's signature. We would have to cut them off after two hours because that's all the time we had, and then we would have police officers escort Coach Bowden out of the area. Otherwise, people would follow him right out the door.

Imagine, for two solid hours he would sign his name just as fast as I could shove the items into his face. He would always want to know if the items were for somebody. He didn't want to just sign something. It was so funny—I would also write down the person's name so he knew who the thing was for, and those people would yell at me, "I don't want Mrs. Bowden to autograph that." I would look up at them and tell them, trying not to get angry, that I was *not* Mrs. Bowden.

REQUEST OVERLOAD

Couples used to think Coach Bowden could marry them because he preached a lot. One guy drove all the way from Texas, bringing his fiancee. He was a huge FSU fan, and he thought Coach Bowden could marry them. I mean, here was a case of a total stranger driving in from Texas, thinking Coach Bowden could just take time to perform a marriage. And he just expected this could happen. But Coach Bowden's just a lay preacher—he can't marry people. So our team chaplain, Clint

Purvis, came in, and we did the ceremony with Coach Bowden as the best man.

We'd get calls before Coach Bowden took his annual cruise with coaches and boosters. These would be calls from people who were going to be on the cruise and who wanted him to marry them. I would tell them, "He can't do that. He's not an ordained minister." Well, they had all these big plans. So guess who married them—me. I am qualified as a notary to perform a marriage ceremony.

Sometimes I would get marriage requests directly, because people thought if I did it, then it would be the same as Coach Bowden doing it. That put me in a unique position. When people found out he couldn't do it, they'd say, "You do it then."

Game days were very busy. Coach Bowden would let writers and columnists from newspapers come up to his office for interviews hours before the game. Or we would have tours through the building. He'd open his door and let people come visit with him. Can you imagine that? The day of a game, and Coach Bowden was visiting with these people.

If we played a game at three thirty, for example, this parade of people would start anywhere from nine o'clock in the morning up until two and a half hours before game time. He would still see people that close to a game. Amazing, isn't it?

Also during the season, the requests for tickets were unbelievable. People would call, claiming to be a good friend or a distant relative who needed three tickets for the Florida game. And they wanted them free and asked whether we could send them. People even thought Coach Bowden could get tickets to NFL playoff games or the Super Bowl or other college games. These requests came from friends and total strangers, and sometimes I would hustle to get tickets for people who Coach Bowden did know and tried to accommodate.

The funny thing is that even as communication improved and cell phones became available, Coach Bowden still asked for me by yelling out of his office. We had an intercom, but he never really learned how to work it. He had no interest in it. A cell phone? Forget it. He would just say, "Sue, Sue!" And if I wasn't in the office, he would go walking down the hall, yelling my name.

Modern technology just went over his head. He did things the old-fashioned way.

BEING PREPARED FOR ANYTHING

Most of the time, he would be watching film or reviewing the game plan. Even though the game plan would already have been put to bed, he would still look over stuff. He kept his note cards, all his game plans, and what he did during the day in neat files. He still has those. He's very organized that way. He's kept every one.

He always had respect for the media. He said, "I will always talk to the media, because they have a job to do also." He felt the same way about the players talking to the media too. He said, "The students are here to learn, and this also is part of their learning process, to be able to talk to the press." It was something that I respected him for.

During football season, he didn't see anybody unless the matter was football related. No other matters. It was the same way he approached playing golf. Every summer, right after Fourth of July, his golf clubs went up in storage and didn't come out again. I don't know how you cut off something that you love like he does, but he totally did. If someone called him, wanting to play golf, he would tell them no. For him, golf was over with, and he strictly got into football.

During the season, he would speak at churches. That's the way he looked at things. He said, "I'll always go to a church, and I always do Fellowship of Christian Athletes," and those things he did free. And if we had an open date, he would permit me to fill the open dates with speaking engagements.

As you can imagine, I didn't have days off—sometimes, not even nights off. I did correspondence at home on Sundays. I would say to people I had a "24-hour-a-day job."

One night at 1:00 a.m., the phone rang. It was Coach Bowden. He was stuck in Texas. He was supposed to fly to Atlanta, and our state aircraft was to pick him up there.

He said, "Sue, I'm stuck in Texas. My connecting plane is late. Tell the pilots in Atlanta not to leave me."

Well, I didn't have the name of the airport or any other information at home. After that, I learned to take it all home. But in this case, I woke up my husband, threw on some clothes, and went out in the middle of the night to the football office to look up the information. I called, and sure enough, the state aircraft was sitting there, and the pilots thought there had been a mistake, that maybe Coach Bowden was on another plane, but they did wait on him.

Another night, he called in the middle of the night and said, "Sue, my car won't start. What do I do?" I knew what he was talking about because he was in a courtesy car. I said, "I'll call the Ford dealership in town." I had an after-hours number—and the dealership took care of it.

HANDLING THE ROUGH TIMES

When we lost a football game, it was not a good time. He would usually be in a bad mood for a couple of days. My rule was to stay clear of him—tiptoe around like you're not bothering him. I never bothered him. He would be angry. The man is a winner; he wanted to win. It didn't matter if it was football, golf, or tic-tac-toe. I knew how competitive he was. He didn't sleep at night. Losses ate at him. He would not be a happy camper, so I learned not to waste his time.

But I was also there for our two national championships and all those big road wins when nobody had heard much about Florida State, and then he was a jolly fellow, great to work around. Cakes and pies and cookies came into our office.

During the season, however, he stayed on a good diet. I went and got his lunch every day. He liked to be kept on vegetables and non-fattening food. We kept him on a balanced meal, but when he was stressed out, I would give him chocolate. It's funny how we do things like that. He never went to the training table himself. He knew if he ever went in there, he would eat every cookie on the counter.

I had such an admiration for him. It was a wonderful time for me. It was very stressful, but it was a wonderful time. I was 62 years old when I decided to leave, so if I hadn't enjoyed it, I would not have stayed.

Every time an assistant coach would leave, we would get hundreds of calls and requests from coaches all over the country who wanted to work for him. It was unbelievable some of the résumés that would come in. Thank goodness there wasn't a lot of staff turnover.

His appeal was huge. You almost hated when it was Christmas or his birthday, because the mail was unbelievable. And the birthday cards he would get—total strangers sending cards. And he would thank all of them.

Coach Bowden's memory is unbelievable. That's something I was in awe of. A young man would write and want to come and work for him as a grad assistant, and Coach Bowden would say, "Oh, I remember, you played against Purdue in that game," or "You were in that Tennessee game against so-and-so." How could he remember this young coach playing in a game that had nothing to do with Florida State? But he did. That shows you the intensity of how closely he watched games.

LOOKING BACK WITH FOND MEMORIES

I never really realized what it meant to work at Florida State or what it meant working for Coach Bowden until after I left and became the president of our FSU Letterman's Club and would visit other clubs.

The first year, I went out to Arizona for the national convention. Each of the schools had a little table that was designed to set up any information you wanted to bring from your school and put it out there. I had a bunch of hats, and I had Coach Bowden sign them, along with a bunch of other things. I had never been to one of these conventions before, so I had no idea what to expect. All of the other tables for schools had these hats and stuff on them.

Well, I could not even get the stuff out of the box before people snatched it all up. Everything was gone, all the hats, everything. All I had left was a color brochure of Coach Bowden, and some woman at another club came up to me and said her son loved Bobby Bowden and asked if she could have it. Then I had nothing left, and the event was just starting. Everything I had was gone. But that shows you the awe of people about Florida State. I really got the sense of how much people loved Bobby Bowden.

You don't realize it when you're there. I didn't realize it. But everybody wanted to hear what we were doing. And just look how our school has grown. We had 18,000 students when I started. Now we have, what, more than 39,000 enrolled?

It was hard work, but don't get me wrong, it was a wonderful time. I will cherish it forever.

RANDY ORAVETZ

THE HEALER

When he's patrolling the sideline during games, often near Bobby Bowden, Randy Oravetz hopes he won't be needed. The best game is an injury-free game for Oravetz, who begins the 2006 season in his 21st year as head athletic trainer and director of sports medicine at Florida State.

Prior to his current role, Oravetz worked at FSU under the direction of beloved trainer Don Fauls. Fauls was seeking some new student trainers in 1976 and interviewed Oravetz, who was then a junior in college. Oravetz has remained at FSU ever since.

As Oravetz readily jokes, one of his primary roles during games, when it's not tense or injury-related, is to stand alongside Coach Bowden and "make him look tall next to me."

Oravetz has stood tall as one of the nation's leading collegiate sports trainers. A former baseball player, his love for that sport was passed on to his son, Tommy, who just completed his freshman season on FSU's baseball team.

Randy Oravetz has been part of the FSU football program since Bowden's arrival. The two have a warm relationship that carries beyond football duties.

I've really been fortunate. My whole career at Florida State has coincided with Coach Bowden's time here. I was a junior in college when I starting working on the training staff in August 1976. That was also the first season with Coach Bowden.

Back then, he coached the quarterbacks. There was no tower over the practice fields. Coach Bowden was always on the field, pointing things out. He was just full of energy all the time.

He was constantly communicating with people and his assistant coaches. But again, at that point, it was a completely new group of people. There were a lot of new faces on the coaching staff.

We didn't have a lot of players who became NFL first-round draft picks, so there was a lot of coaching going on back then. It was more a matter of trying to get the right guys in the right position. It was more a matter of trying to find out who was a good player.

Before the 1979 season, as the program started to develop, Coach Bowden told all the players, "We're going to put our name on the map." Sure enough, it happened.

From the get-go, Coach Bowden developed a reputation for a tough football team. Yeah, we did a little bit of razzle-dazzle, and yeah, we had some trick plays, but we pretty much lined up and beat other teams.

There was a lot of pounding, pounding, pounding in practices. More so than now, because back then Florida State maybe had one player good enough to merit being a first-round draft pick. The talent level was so different.

In those early years, Coach Bowden was very involved in practice. There was a lot of hands-on coaching. He was full of energy. He stuck his nose everywhere, jumping around from station to station.

In the practices, there were a lot more one-on-one type of drills—the Oklahoma drills, Texas drills. The practices were very hard, and there was a lot of pounding going on.

The coaches were trying to find tough guys. They had a lot of mediocre players, and they were trying to find the toughest ones who could battle. Guys like Scott Warren, Paul Piurowski, Reggie Herring—those are the guys who ended up playing for four years.

Coach Bowden basically said, in effect, "These are the guys we're going to win with." With all the tough practices, those guys proved they could handle it. They did what the coaches were trying to accomplish.

Because of the tough practices, all the hitting, there were more bone fractures, a lot more concussions that we treated as a medical staff. And, of course, the type of helmet we use nowadays is different. Helmets are much better now. But those days were more of a pounding era.

Now I think we just have better athletes, so the practices are structured differently. Back then, spring practices were 20 days and with full gear every day. Now they're only 15 days, and the amount of days in full gear is restricted. Back then it was 20 days going all out. The coaches had T-shirts made saying, "Tough 20." When you made it through all 20 practices, you got a shirt. And you really earned it.

BOWDEN'S TOWERING PRESENCE

I can laugh about it now, but when we were on the field back then, we had to always be looking for Coach Bowden. We never knew when he was standing right behind us, so we made sure to keep our mouths shut and didn't say certain things.

Now that he's up on the tower, you know where he is all the time, so there is a lot more stuff being yelled back and forth on the field. For example, when players would be cussing or saying stuff to each other, Coach Bowden would yell, "What are you saying, son?" Now, when he's in the tower, some things don't quite get heard up there.

Although you don't see Coach Bowden as hands-on during practice, believe me, in the staff meeting he's very hands-on. He's up there demonstrating on the blackboard; he's getting on those coaches; he's asking point-blank questions to them. So he's still very involved, but in a different way.

During practices, Coach Bowden keeps index cards in his pocket, along with a pen or pencil. When he sees something he doesn't like or wants to ask the coaches about, he immediately writes it down on the card. It's amazing how much information he can get on a 5×7 index card, but there is a lot of information on it.

And the next day, in that staff meeting, he goes down every bit of that information with those coaches. It doesn't matter whether it's defense, offense, or kicking he's going to ask the coaches about. Back in his earlier years, a lot of that was done on field.

In the morning staff meetings, as head trainer, I give the coaches updates on every injury. I was introduced to those staff meetings around 1980. Don Fauls was our head trainer back then, but he wanted me to go into the meetings for experience because he knew I needed to learn how it was done.

It was definitely interesting. The coaches asked a lot of questions, so Don had to be sharp on his feet. Don Fauls was well-respected, so the coaches pretty much trusted what he said. In that role, if you're in front of a group of coaches and you start stuttering about player injuries or status, they're going to eat you up.

But you also have to know what's good for the athlete and what's good for the football team. Sometimes, you've got to protect that athlete. There are times, both then and now, when I might have to hold a guy out of practice or limit him because of circumstances in his life unrelated to a physical injury. The coaches don't necessarily need to know about that stuff right then. A lot of times it's personal stuff—things like a mom who has cancer, a girlfriend being pregnant—something of that nature is going on. I've got to handle it.

The old saying around the team is, "When all else fails, call Randy." That philosophy helped me in a lot of relationships with Coach Bowden and players. One of the funniest was with tailback Sammie Smith during the late 1980s.

Sammie had missed six Tuesday practices in a row. Those are the toughest practices, the most physical practices of a game week. Sammie did not like contact. He would have the worst injuries ever, in his mind, after every football game. On Monday he couldn't practice. Tuesday—he couldn't practice. Wednesday—he would only be able to jog around, and by Thursday, he would have a miraculous recovery.

We called them MRs, miraculous recoveries.

There would be a lot of times on a Tuesday when Sammie couldn't practice with pads on. He would say, "I can run, but my shoulder is really bothering me." If not his shoulder, it would be his hand. He would tell me he couldn't hold onto the ball.

Sammie would come into the training room, moping around, dragging his leg, saying his hamstring was killing him—all that kind of

Veteran Director of Sports Medicine Randy Oravetz has seen Bobby Bowden deal with the violent side of football. *Courtesy of FSU Sports Information*

stuff. So, of course, I had to always tell Coach Bowden about Sammie's status for practice. Coach Bowden stayed pretty patient with him.

I swear, I think Sammie had a book that told him all the right symptoms for each injury. Sort of like yes for this, no for that. Yes, no, yes, no—like a word association after each injury.

On the seventh week, after Sammie had missed six straight Tuesday practices, I messed up. I found Sammie out practicing on a Monday night. All the players were around and in a huddle, and I yelled, "Sammie, that's incredible! You're going to be able to practice tomorrow. Why, there's nothing wrong with you.

"The only way you'll get out of practicing tomorrow is if you're in the hospital."

Well, I'll be darned, that next day, say around 2:30 in the afternoon, an hour before we're going to start practice, I got a call from a hospital in town. Sammie had checked himself into the hospital.

I got a call from the emergency room, telling me Sammie was there. He claimed he was having a heart attack. They told me Sammie was saying he was having heart palpitations. Of course, there was nothing wrong with him, but I had to go there and get him out and tell the coaches Sammie wasn't going to be at practice. They screamed at me, saying, "If you wouldn't have said anything last night, he would be here!"

On the opposite end of Sammie—and these guys played at the same time—was Deion Sanders. Without a doubt, he was one of the toughest guys of all time. Deion missed one practice in four years. It's one of the many reasons why Coach Bowden loved Deion Sanders. He loved his toughness, his work ethic. Deion reminded him of his era, only with incredible talent and speed. I mean there was no comparison in the athletic ability between the different eras, but Deion was old-school about practicing.

Deion practiced harder than maybe any of the athletes in the history of Florida State. There's a reason why Deion was so great. He worked at what he did.

Deion forced the issue with a lot of guys; he would yell at them to suck it up. He used to get on Sammie, yelling at him, "Sammie, you're not hurt. Let's go!"

OLD-SCHOOL MENTALITY

I always joke with Coach Bowden about this, but when he talks about the old days, back when he played, he was like the toughest player ever.

He'll say to me, "Randy, I used to play with this or that. Nobody ever sat out practice. Now, Randy, a guy gets a torn fingernail and you let him out." Of course, it's not that way. But coaches are coaches. It's funny with coaches or former players. The older they get, the tougher they were in their minds.

They tend to forget when they were 20 and what things felt like. Plus, these kids are away from home, and a lot of them have never been yelled at. They were the prima donnas of their high school teams, and they've never been yelled at or told to play through injury, so we deal with some of those issues.

That's not the way it was when Coach Bowden and a lot of our coaches played high school football. Coach Bowden and a lot of our other coaches, they're old-school. When they played college football, they played in a different era. Football is football, but there are different eras of football: the '50s versus the '70s versus the '90s versus 2000. They're all different eras.

Back then, yes, guys played with fractures, and sometimes it was said the player had a sprained ankle rather than a fracture on his leg. But you've got to remember, back then players weren't running the 40 in 4.4 seconds like they do now. Linebackers and defensive tackles weren't running 4.4 or 4.5. Everybody was about the same speed. Back then there were also 150 guys on a team. There might have been six quarterbacks on a team, so that third-, fourth-, and fifth-string quarterback was getting pounded in practice because the team could afford to do it.

It's just not that way anymore. Plus the players are different because society is different. In our role as trainers, we often have to butter up the players. So we've got a split duty. We deal with coaches, who want the players available, and the kids, who are often not used to being injured.

In those staff meetings, there is often a lot of banter going on between the coaches and me. There's a lot of discussion about a player.

Luckily, I've been around a while, so the coaches know I'm not feeding them a line. We're to the point now where I can tell the coaches and they believe me. I will say to them, for example, "This guy will be only 75 percent on Saturday. That's all he's going to be. He can't be more than 75-percent capacity."

So the coaches have to decide, Is the guy's backup, who will be playing at 90 percent, better than the 75-percent guy? That's the trade-off. You take an injury like a hamstring; that doesn't get better. It doesn't just rapidly heal. Sometimes you just have to shut a guy down, keep him from practicing or playing to avoid making it far worse and to get the injured player back before the season ends.

The coaches will ask me, for example, "Can this guy play with a broken hand?"

"Well, yeah, but he'll be playing with only one arm. Is that what you want?" Those are some of the discussions we have.

Coach Bowden is really good about it. He really watches a player. Sometimes he'll put pressure on a kid to push forward, but he also knows we've got to protect players. Coach Bowden wants them to be tough; he wants them to be macho, but if the kid is not ready, for his protection, he's going to listen to what we have to say.

Our team doctors, Dr. Tom Haney, Dr. Doug Henderson, and Dr. Kris Stowers have been around a long time. They've made good decisions about when to hold a kid from playing.

Sometimes Coach Bowden will get animated about injuries because he wants a certain player in the lineup. I'll say, "Coach we're working with him twice a day, three times a day. The kid is giving us good effort. And that's all we can ask."

Now, if a player is not giving us good effort in the training room to rehab an injury, we'll let Coach Bowden get on him about it. Some kids are just not mentally tough. They just kind of fade, and when they have injuries and have never been hurt before, it's tough.

We've had games where a lot of guys get hurt at once. Probably the worst was in October 1991 in a game at LSU. It was pouring rain. We went in there with an undefeated team, heading toward what we hoped was a national title season.

We had 16 guys who started that game but did not finish. That was like our Waterloo, so to speak. On that Monday I had to walk into the coaches' meetings and say, "This guy has a broken elbow; this guy has a torn-up knee; this guy has a compound fracture; this guy has this." Coach Bowden just looked at me with a stunned expression.

He just couldn't believe it. He said, "Randy, you can't be telling me this. We have Miami and Florida coming up." That year, Florida State played Miami in the second to last game, then Florida in the last game of the season, back to back. I knew the situation.

I said, "Coach, this is what we've got. I'm trying to tell you, this is where we are. There is no miracle cure."

Well, that game, all those injuries, wound up costing us an undefeated season and our first national championship. Fortunately, we were able to come back two years later, with Charlie Ward at quarterback, and win it all.

BOWDEN AND WEINKE

Probably one of the scarier injuries I've dealt with occurred with quarterback Chris Weinke in 1998. We were playing in November at home against Virginia, and Chris had his neck jammed while getting hit on a sack.

We didn't know immediately what it was, but we had some ideas. It was a big concern. As the X-rays later showed, there was a crack in his vertebrae. Coach Bowden was very concerned about his health.

He kept asking that day, "Is he going to be all right? Can he walk? Will he be permanently paralyzed?" I told him if we didn't operate immediately, he could be paralyzed.

Chris came through the operation fine, but it was a long road back. The next year, as we were getting Chris ready to play, there were a lot of concerns on how we were going to do this. We made an agreement with Coach Bowden that he could not do a quarterback sneak anymore with Chris Weinke behind center. We could not take any risks out there.

So, as that season showed, how many times did our No. 2 quarterback, Marcus Outzen, come in and run that play? A lot. And that's why we did it.

But in the national title game against Virginia Tech, we put Marcus in there, and Virginia Tech was thinking it was going to be a quarterback sneak. Instead, Marcus took off on a bootleg run and picked up about 12 yards to keep a scoring drive alive. That proved to be a very big play in that game.

The thing we laugh about now, when Chris went into the NFL with the Carolina Panthers, he was doing quarterback sneaks. It was like they were saying, "OK, Chris, you're in the NFL. We don't care."

Coach Bowden knew Weinke was a mature young man who was going to give him everything he had, but Coach also knew we had to back off how we used him. Coach Bowden also knew the risks of a neck injury.

What people didn't know is that once Chris got through the initial part of his recovery, we began practicing every day indoors—just him and me. We threw the football indoors for about four or five weeks. We didn't want anybody else knowing it. But we did it to get his psyche ready for practice.

So when he did come out for practice that winter before the '99 spring practice, he impressed a lot of people right off the bat. Chris then led us to a perfect season and a national championship. The next year, he won the Heisman Trophy. It was awesome that he was capable of doing what he did. He's one of the all-time special guys.

Most of the players are great about dealing with injuries. Luckily, I think guys on the team see what other teammates have done. They see how others have fought to get back on the field. They see how others have done rehab and that they've gotten back up. When it's a torn ACL or a sprain, the players learn from each other. So we've had a lot of good examples of guys who take care of business, who knew what it took to get back out there.

Coach Bowden cares about each player and the injuries. At the same time, he also knows he may have to move on to the next guy. It's part of our business. Let's face it, football is a violent sport. People do not realize the amount of injuries, the amount of hurt, the amount of discomfort a player has to go through.

In this sport, if things are discomforting, then you're playing football. If not, then you're watching. If you're out there playing, you're getting banged up.

I think what's happened now, as opposed to when I first started at Florida State, is we've got more players here, better players. So there's not as great of a step down from the first-team guy to the second-team guy. In the mid-'80s, when you went from a first-team guy to a second-team guy, there was a huge drop-off in talent and ability. It was tough to have some of those front-line guys sit on the bench and try to protect them.

But just like now, if they weren't ready, they didn't play.

SIDELINE SITUATIONS

Coach Bowden always seems to be ready for any situation.

Right before the Florida State–Miami game in 1989 in Tallahassee, the team was out on the field warming up. The stadium was in a frenzy. It was a night game, Miami was ranked No. 1, and everybody was fired up.

Coach Bowden was in the locker room taking a nap.

This is right before the game, and I came in, looked over, and saw his hat flopping up and down with his head. Coach Bowden's head of security was in the locker room, and he gave me this look of "What do we do?" And I said, "I'm not going to wake him up."

Well, sure enough, the players all started coming into the locker room, and they were all hootin' and hollerin'. The first 10 or 20 players who came in looked over at Coach Bowden.

Then all of a sudden, Coach Bowden kind of stood up. He woke up and looked ready to go. All the players kind of looked at his demeanor and said, in effect, "Well, if Coach Bowden is relaxed, we ought to be relaxed." Everybody was like, "If he's OK, we're OK. He's cool, calm, and collected." And the thing is, Coach Bowden didn't intend it to be that way; that was just him. But the players fed off his relaxed attitude.

Then we went out and put a whoopin' on Miami that night.

Coach Bowden has always been careful not to get people too fired up too soon. That's the thing people don't understand about the national championship game. From the time of warmups to the end of the game, that's almost a five-hour ball game. You cannot be emotionally up for that long.

Coach Bowden has been through a lot of games. He knows when to get his teams revved up. He keeps a nice demeanor on the sideline. He's always telling the guys, "This is the one. This is the one."

Coach Bowden is just as revved up about the first game of a season as he is for the last game. He loves football. He loves coaching. He likes dealing with young men and molding those young men. He loves seeing former players and hugging them. He remembers their moms, and he'll say things like, "Is she still making that blueberry pie?" He remembers what a player's mom made for him on a recruiting trip years ago. It's amazing how he remembers stuff like that.

Coach can be very, very intense, and he can be very relaxed. He can step back and analyze. I think early in his career, he was very intense. Now he analyzes and steps back more. Some of the things you see on the sideline, that's just Bobby Bowden. What you see is what you get. That's him.

It's not about him. It's about Florida State football, and he'll be the first one to step up and accept responsibility when things aren't going right. He takes the blame. But I've also seen when we're winning, and he credits the players.

He sticks up for his players. He's saved a lot more kids than we've ever had to let go. He's straightened a lot of kids out, and they've become great men. Coach Bowden is an honest, caring man. That's the bottom line. He loves coaching. He loves dealing with young athletes.

People have no idea how many times I've had to go up to his office with a player, whether they've had some personal problems or family problems, or made poor decisions. And Coach Bowden will handle that.

In my opinion, he has put Florida State on the map in every sort of way. The growth that has occurred on this campus, it's because of him. The national exposure has all been about Bobby Bowden. Before Bobby Bowden, yeah, we had some good teams with Coach Bill Peterson here, and we had some other good teams with different coaches, but when Bobby Bowden got here, all of a sudden, Tallahassee became noted.

When you see what this campus at FSU looked like when I got here in 1976 and what it looks like now, there's no comparison. To see what this stadium looks like—it's no comparison. To see us go through an airport to go anywhere and see people wearing Florida State jerseys, that didn't happen in the '70s. I don't care if I'm in the Caribbean or in Oregon, people know Florida State.

Coach Bowden put Tallahassee on the map. The football program made the community grow. I know it made the university grow.

I think that is what Coach Bowden has meant to Florida State.

ROB WILSON

─◦──◦──◦──

THE STORYTELLER

Since arriving at Florida State in 1987 as an assistant sports informa-tion director (SID), he has been known for his storytelling and believe-it-or-not experiences. He can light up a banquet room with many of his tales. In addition to assuming the duties of his new position as associate athletic director, Wilson has been active in coordinating football media operations for the past 15 years. He has been around Bobby Bowden for national title wins and deflating losses.

Twice I met Bobby Bowden for the first time. The funniest may have been upon my return to FSU in July 1987 after accepting a full-time position in the sports information office.

I had been a graduate assistant in sports information in 1982 and 1983, so Coach Bowden had seen me around before. Then I went to East Carolina and worked for that school's sports information depart-ment before I came back to FSU. My first weekend on the job was the Fourth of July weekend in 1987.

It was the Monday after the holiday, and everyone was still on holi-day break. The whole Moore Athletic Center building was basically empty; no one was around, including my boss. I had no idea what to do.

A documentary on Coach Bowden had just been completed for a public broadcasting network. Lisa Franson, the assistant SID at the time, met me and said, "Hey, why don't you go watch this tape on Coach Bowden? It's really cool."

She said, "Coach is out of town. Why don't you just go watch it in his office?"

So I went down and sat in his office. It was the middle of the afternoon, and I was behind his desk, watching this documentary. I don't think I had my feet up on his desk, but I was real close to doing that. Then, all of a sudden, the door opened, and in walked Coach Bowden.

Now, (a) he didn't know anyone was in there in the first place; and (b), he really had no idea who I was. I was sitting there mortified. I wanted to disappear like water down a drain—just drift away.

But I jumped up, saying, "Coach, I'm sorry. I'm sorry."

He said, "Hey, hey, I'm not going to be here long, just stay right there."

I tried to get up, but he pushed me back down in his seat. He was just getting some stuff off of his desk.

He said, "Hey, good to see you." He had kind of recognized me.

I told him I was back working in sports information, and he said, "Hey, stay right there, no problem."

He fiddled around with some stuff for about five minutes, got what he needed, then left and said, "See you later."

I met him the first time back when I was a graduate assistant. I had gone out to football practice that day to get some post-practice quotes from him. I happened to have been wearing a white golf shirt. Bad mistake. Coach loved to chew tobacco back then. As I was talking to him, tobacco juice flew out from his mouth. When I got back to the fraternity house where I lived, I looked at the shirt; it was just covered in tobacco juice spots.

I didn't wash the shirt. I kept it for a long time as a trophy. I learned then, never wear white around Coach Bowden.

SPOILING DINNER

Those two encounters may have been funny, but they weren't the most embarrassing time around Coach. That happened a couple years after I had gone to work full-time.

Few associated with Florida State can match Assistant Athletic Director Rob Wilson, seen here with Bowden and Billy Smith, when it comes to telling Bowden stories. *Courtesy of Ryals Lee, FSU Photo Lab*

There was a basketball writer from New York, a freelance writer, who was going to do a regional magazine and was going to incorporate Florida State in it. Of course, the magazine never got off the ground, but the writer was this fast-talking New York guy. So he came in, and former FSU basketball coach Pat Kennedy said to me, "You need to take him out to dinner," and all that good stuff.

So I met him, and the guy was literally living out of his car, going to all of these places. He had just been to Auburn. He was going to be at FSU for a day. Then he was going down to Florida, trying to get everybody to buy into this thing. He was about as Yankee as you can get. I mean the talk, the accent, the looks, the style, the speed at which he moved—everything.

So I took him to this restaurant in Tallahassee called the Brothers Three. Back then it was *the* restaurant to eat at.

The guy said to me, "I haven't eaten in two days." He claimed he just hadn't had time to eat, and I'd already figured out I didn't want to be around this guy too much longer.

We sat down at the restaurant, and this guy ordered two meals. He ordered a fish meal and a steak meal. Then he went to the salad bar, which was a huge area in the middle of the restaurant.

Now, bear in mind, this was a restaurant where state senators and all the rest of the who's who of Tallahassee often ate. The writer headed up to the salad bar, and I heard him yelling, "Hey, they've got these olives here. These olives are $5.99 a pound in New York. You can have all you want here."

He came back, and his plate was huge. There was lettuce falling off the plate. I was just mortified and praying I didn't see anybody I knew in there. And he was talking the whole time he was eating. There was ranch dressing going everywhere. Of course, by then, everybody in the restaurant knew he was there.

So our meal came, and at the same time, there was a disturbance in the restaurant. You could tell something was going on. I looked up, and in came Coach Bowden. He didn't have his wife, Ann, with him, but he was with another couple, and they were coming in for dinner.

Luckily, this writer had his back to Coach Bowden. I was praying he wouldn't turn around while the staff sat Coach Bowden and his friends in the other room.

I was thinking, "OK, phew. Thank God. I've dodged a bullet there."

Well, this guy finished his meals and, sure enough, he went back to the salad bar for more. And then he saw Coach Bowden. Earlier that day, I had introduced him to Coach, and it had been one of those brief meetings where Coach had looked at me and sort of rolled his eyes.

The writer went over to Coach Bowden's table, and the whole restaurant was watching. He'd also had about four or five cocktails, so he was both tipsy and obnoxious.

I heard him yelling in that thick New York accent, "Coach, Coach, your record is unbelievable. . . . It's unbelievable your record. And you won so many games.

"Coach, it's kinda like this. . . . It's like you're [having sex with] Marilyn Monroe. After a while, it's just [sex]."

At that point, I wrestled him out of the restaurant, and we headed on our way. I was embarrassed beyond belief. The next morning, as I was walking into the building, Coach was coming in at exactly the same time, and I was thinking, "Oh no, what is he going to say?"

He looked up at me and said, "Hey, I bet I had a better night than you did last night."

I will never forget that.

EVEN THE PRESIDENT IS A BUDDY

When we won the second national championship on January 4, 2000, against Virginia Tech in the Sugar Bowl, we spent the last minute of the game knowing we were going to win it. When we got to the locker room afterward, somebody I didn't know walked up to me and said, "The president is on the phone."

I said, "OK, we'll be right with you." I was thinking he meant the university president.

The guy said, "No, no. It's the president."

Then it hit me—*the president.* He meant President Clinton. So I went to Billy Smith, Bowden's security officer, and said, "Billy, the president is on the phone."

He ran right in and grabbed Coach, who took the call in a little closet that had a phone in it. Coach went in there, and I was thinking, "This is a hell of an opportunity." So I went in there with him to hear what he was saying.

I could only hear Coach's part of the conversation. The first thing he said to the president of the United States was, "Hey, buddy, why aren't you working tonight?" And then they went on and on.

Finally he said, "Well, thank you, buddy," and he hung up. Billy Smith and I looked at each other and said, "He just talked to the president of the United States and said, 'Hey, buddy.'"

Later that year we went to the White House. We had also gone after winning our first national championship six years earlier. So we were the first team to visit in Clinton's presidency and the last team he had at the White House.

I was impressed with Clinton because he asked for 15 minutes—and wound up taking 20 minutes—to speak only with the players. There was nobody else in their meeting except the team. No cheerleaders, no coaches—just the players and the president.

President Clinton had already talked with Coach in the Oval Office for about 20 minutes. I later heard it was a deep discussion too, because this was post–Monica Lewinsky. But during the meeting with the team, Clinton talked to our players, and he challenged them all to take what they had been given and reminded them they were role models. I thought that was a big deal.

WHAT'S RECEIVED IN VEGAS, LEAVES VEGAS

Probably the most amazing time I've spent with Coach Bowden is the time we were invited to the ESPY Awards in Las Vegas. It was the winter of 2000 and the 10th anniversary of the ESPYs. They were naming the team of the decade, team of the year—all that stuff.

Now, Coach Bowden is not big on Las Vegas, and Ann doesn't like it all. Obviously, he doesn't like gambling. In fact, he thinks gambling is one of the worst things you can do.

But ESPN kept calling and saying, "We really hope Coach is going to go. We've got Burt Reynolds as one of the presenters." I knew then we were going to win one of the awards.

I went up to Coach's office and said, "Coach, we really need to go to this thing."

He said, "Yeah, they're giving me two airline tickets. Do you want to go?"

I said, "Yeah, I'll go."

He said, "OK, you make all the arrangements. I want the last plane in and the first plane out."

Well, as fate had it, I got bumped off my flight and ended up on the same flight with Coach. It was really fun to travel with him. We were in first class, and I could see all the people nudging each other, saying, "Hey, that's Coach Bowden."

We sat down, and the fight attendant said, "Coach, would you like something to drink?"

And he said, "No, but you can start that snack basket around whenever you like." Everybody in first class laughed, because they had been wondering what he would say.

When we landed in Las Vegas, we figured we'd just get a cab to the hotel. Nope, there was a valet holding one of those cardboard signs that read, "Bowden." We hopped in his limo and headed toward the MGM Grand, where we were staying.

As we drove past the main entrance of the complex, we asked the driver, "Hey, isn't this the lobby?" and the driver said, "No, you have to go to the celebrity entrance." So we went around to the back of the hotel, and sure enough, there was a back door. The driver let us out, and there was a line of celebrities waiting to check in. I could already tell this was serious.

When I got to my room, the phone was already ringing.

I was thinking, "Who would be calling me?"

It was Coach. He said, "Hey, Rob, do you have a bunch of gifts in your room?"

I looked around my room and told him I didn't have anything.

He said, "Well, you got to get up here." So I went up to his room, where he had propped the door open. He was sitting in the easy chair, just kind of laughing. I turned the corner, and there were two double beds. One of the beds was just covered in gifts—I mean covered with all kinds of stuff. And he was laughing.

He asked me, "How am I going to get all this stuff back to Tallahassee?"

I started looking through the stuff.

One of the gifts was a leather gym bag. I opened the bag, and it had every EA Sports video game you could think of inside of it. There must have been 70 of them in the bag.

He asked, "What's that?"

I said, "Oh, they're just sports video games. You won't want these."

He said, "What? I've got grandkids. That's perfect. Put those down. I'll take those home."

I opened the next bag, which was a leather backpack that would have made a good prop in a vampire movie. It was just this futuristic thing, but inside were all these hemp hair-care products.

So he asked, "What's that?"

I said, "It's shampoo made out of marijuana."

He asked, "Is that legal?"

"Do you want it?" I asked back.

"Oh yeah."

Then there was a bag with all these golf shirts. There must have been one in his size for every golf course in Las Vegas. There was another bag that had a bunch of stuff, including a can of tennis balls. So I opened the can and threw the tennis balls in the trash can.

He asked, "What are you doing?"

I said, "Coach, that's just a can of tennis balls. These tennis balls are, like, a $1.80 at Eckerd's."

He said, "I've got grandkids. . . . I need to have those."

Then he stopped me and said, "Rob, all the alcohol is yours—even the tequila. See, bet you didn't think I knew what tequila was, did you?"

So we started packing all this stuff. He wouldn't let me throw anything away. We split it up so we could get it on the airplane.

The show was around seven o'clock that night. We had to be in our rooms at a specific time, and the show organizers were set to call our rooms and let us know when we had to come down. I think we had to be there at 5:00 p.m. for a show that started two hours later.

I was thinking, "Man, what the hell are we going to do for two hours?"

They called Coach, and he called me, and we went down together. On his floor, there was a private celebrity elevator. We got on the elevator, and we went down to the first floor. But instead of walking out to where the show was, some people started walking us to the front door.

They put us in a limo just to ride around to the back of the hotel. There was James Caan waiting for his limo, and Joe Theisman was right next to us. Coach was telling the organizers, "The show venue is right there. I can see it. Why don't we just go walk over there?"

But that was not how they wanted to do it.

Joe Theisman decided he was going to get in our limo because he knew Coach, and the three of us pulled around to the back of the hotel. It was like the entrance at the Academy Awards. There were probably about 500 or 600 people watching as people arrived. They had stands built out there. There was a red carpet with all kinds of TV crews and fashion reporters, and we had no idea it was going to be this big of a deal.

Now, I was really sweating bullets, thinking, "In a couple seconds, these limo doors are going to open in front of all these people, and it's going to be Joe Theisman, Bobby Bowden, and—oh, who is this other guy?"

I decided I was just going to stay in the limo, and when it went back around to the front, I'd come back through the other entrance.

Theisman said, "No, that's not how it's going to happen. You go out first, and wave like you're the king of a country. They won't know the difference."

I got out and started waving, and the flashbulbs went off.

Theisman got out, and then Coach got out. I'll never forget when some fashion reporter asked Coach what kind of tux he was wearing, hoping to hear him say the brand name.

He said, "Well, it's rented. I don't know—have no idea." You know they were expecting him to say Armani or Gucci or one of those designers.

Then we went into this small room, a holding room. When we got in there, there were probably about 20 people in it. But within an hour, it was elbow-to-elbow with every sports celebrity you could ever name. I mean Peyton Manning was standing next to Mario Lemieux, who was standing next to the U.S. women's soccer team, who were standing next to Tiger Woods. I mean the most novice sports fan could have named everybody in that room.

But there were two people that no one could recognize—me and Peyton Manning's future brother-in-law. How we got in there, I'm not really sure.

Coach sat down at a table, and Dick Vermeil came over, and they started talking a million miles an hour about football. Then, in came the now-late Reggie White. He made a beeline for Coach Bowden.

He asked, "Coach, why didn't you recruit me?" And they started going a million a miles an hour.

That table became the center of attention. Jerry Rice, James Caan, and Burt Reynolds came over. There was Dick Vermeil, Reggie White, and Michael Clarke Duncan, the star actor from *The Green Mile*. He was a bundle of energy. He saw Coach and lit up, saying, "Bobby Bowden! Oh, Coach, good to see you."

Coach looked at him and said, "I just saw your movie. I saw it last night. It was a great movie."

Duncan was stunned.

He said, "You saw my movie?" He was so excited, and the two of them kept talking like two kids.

Pretty soon, it came time to leave for the show. As I walked out to look around, a woman came up to me and asked, "Are you Rob Wilson? Come with me."

She took me outside to where the ESPN TV trucks were parked. In them were the college football crews that do our games. They were in hysterics, laughing because they saw me get out of that limo, acting like I was somebody famous. They asked which seat I would be sitting in for the show, and they said, "OK, we'll make sure we cut away to a commercial one time on you."

As Coach and I were going in to the theatre, there came this gorgeous woman walking toward us, looking for Bobby Bowden. It was Cybill Shepherd.

She said, "Coach, I'm just a huge fan of yours," and she gave him a big hug. It was one of the few times I've ever seen Coach Bowden flustered.

He turned to me—I'll never forget this—and said, "Cybill Shepherd sure is a handsome woman." Throughout the night, he kept bringing up Cybill Shepherd, saying how beautiful she looked.

The show went on and on, and it was getting late for us. I was looking at Coach, and he had gotten his ever-present notepad out and was writing things and then scratching them out. I was thinking, "What in the world is he going to say? How do you impress this audience?" A while later, I did one of the stupidest things I've ever done. I made a suggestion to him for how he ought to handle his speech.

I said, "Coach, have you thought about what you are going to say?"

He said, "Yeah, I don't know exactly what I'm going to do."

I said, "Well, maybe you should act like this is no big deal—that Vegas is no different than Tallahassee." And he looked at me like I was some idiot, sort of like a fan suggesting a play on his call-in radio show.

We shared the award that night with the Tennessee Lady Vol basketball team, and when Coach got up there, he said, "It's great to share the stage with Tennessee basketball. I'm a big fan of Coach [Pat] Summitt, and what you have done is incredible."

He then said, "And I would like to thank my wife, Ann. She really has been looking forward to this trip. She has been packed for a couple weeks. But you know how it is, you just can't remember everything."

Then he deadpanned, "Now, I knew I forgot something."

The humor is difficult to convey, but this joke brought the house down. It absolutely brought the house down. Michael Jordan was sitting there doing the ol' knee-slapping; he was laughing so hard. The place was up for grabs. I just marveled at how Coach pulled this off.

It was the delivery and the way he set up the joke. It was so funny that every time they would come back from commercial, the emcee that night, actor Jimmy Smits, picked up on it and would say, "Coach, we found Ann. She's in Sacramento."

After the show ended, I ran into Chris Fowler from ESPN, and he said, "You've got a room full of every sports celebrities and most every other celebrity in this country—and Bobby Bowden has the line of the night. That's all you need to know."

That's what's so great about Coach: he is just the way he appears. That's why it always ticks me off when I hear or read of people claiming he is not genuine. He's got a tremendous sense of humor. He sees humor in everything.

As we left to go back home, I ended up with the funky leather backpack. I knew he might want to give it away, so I left the backpack on his desk back at FSU. I happened to be up in the football office when he picked it up. He walked out of the office, sports coat on, and he had the backpack on his back. He was whistling real loud too so everybody would see him on the way to the elevator.

Carol Moore, the defensive coaches' secretary, said, "Coach, that sure is an interesting backpack you have on."

Without even stopping to think of a comeback, he said, "Camping, Carol. I love camping."

He got on the elevator. I was just in stitches.

GENE DECKERHOFF

THE BROADCASTER

The truly special announcers are the ones who fit name association with a team. Gene Deckerhoff has been that way with Florida State. The former junior college basketball star from Jacksonville began his broadcasting career in 1964. The passion never waned. For the past 30 years he has been the play-by-play voice of Florida State basketball, expanding to football in 1979 when becoming the "Voice of the Seminoles." His first football season was Florida State's undefeated regular season in 1979, which is now symbolic of the success Deckerhoff has enjoyed with FSU athletics. He became one of only four announcers ever inducted into the Florida Sports Hall of Fame. In addition to FSU broadcasts, Deckerhoff has also been the radio voice of the Tampa Bay Buccaneers since 1989. No matter the team or the sport, his excitement permeates through each broadcast.

In terms of football and where Florida State was in its own history, Bobby Bowden was the right man at the right time at the right place. Didn't Winston Churchill say that? I don't know, but maybe Bobby is Florida State's Winston Churchill.

When Bobby came to Florida State, I think that, number one, he related to the area. He was from Alabama, and basically, northwest Florida is lower Alabama. So I think that part clicked. Number two, I really don't think Bobby had ambitions other than being a college football coach. Some coaches don't fit because they want to do other things. They don't feel like coaching college football forever is their place in life. They want to go to the NFL.

But Bobby came in at a time when Florida State needed success or the program was going to go away. Bobby came in during a time when the schedule he was presented was a nightmare. Bobby came in and said, "I think I can make this work, and I'm going to do my best," and he inherited some pretty good players.

I think the first year, in 1976, he basically benched everybody who started the first two or three games and brought in a freshman-sophomore-dominated group and put them around a nucleus of veterans he thought he could trust. They took their lumps, going 5-6 that year, but the next year the team went 10-2, finished nationally ranked, and went to the Tangerine Bowl in Orlando.

I think that season was the jumping-off point where Florida State and Bobby Bowden got married. It was a great marriage, and it's lasted almost forever.

For me, there's an ironic twist to how we first met. I knew Bobby's old house before I knew him.

When my wife, Ann, and I moved to Tallahassee from Bradenton with our three sons in October 1974, I had already made a deposit on a house. I had been up here two times to meet with the new management of a radio station, which back then was WTNT-AM 1270.

Before we moved, however, my wife flat-out refused to live in any house that I had made a deposit on. She didn't trust me that it would be the right house.

So I was thinking, "Well, what are we going do? We've got everything packed. We're set to move." On a Sunday, we start going through the want-ads of the *Tallahassee Democrat*.

We found this place on 920 Maplewood Drive and went to go see the house. Ann liked it. Of course, it was double what we were paying in Bradenton, which I didn't like. But we went ahead and called, and we decided we would rent this house.

The folks who lived on the one side of the house, the man was a professor at Florida State. He and his wife had two sons. The professor had gone to West Virginia to get his doctorate degree.

He says, "You know the fella that owned that house first was a football coach."

I said, "Really?"

He said, "Yeah, he's up at West Virginia now. That's where I got my Ph.D. His name is Bobby Bowden."

So, as it turned out, I rented the house that Bobby Bowden originally owned. Of all the incredible things that could have happened, I moved into his house. Bobby Bowden was the first mortgage holder. I've often reminded Bobby about that.

So we knew we had a connection before he ever came back to Florida State.

THE EARLY YEARS WORKING WITH BOWDEN

I've done his radio shows since 1979. We used to tape after he would speak to the Seminole boosters each Monday at the round Holiday Inn on Tennessee Street. The radio station, WGLF, was right next door, and Bobby would come over after the luncheon, and we would do his pregame show for the next week.

Before I took the job, I didn't really know much about Bobby. All I knew was that people were excited he was here, so that meant I was excited.

Bobby's first game in 1976 occurred just after I had been hired to be sports director of Channel 27. At the time, the station was known as WECA. In fact, the owner's widow still attends FSU games.

The first game Bobby coached was against Memphis State in Memphis. I'll never forget it. I had taken a part-time job at the dog track in Monticello. The fellow who was doing the job full-time was program director at one of the radio stations. He wanted at least one day off. I would go over every Sunday and collect cash and money from him, but I'd do the Saturday shift.

That particular time, I called him and said, "I can't do Saturday." I told him we were having a rehearsal at the station. I think that may be one of the few lies I have ever told in my life. The truth was that I wanted to go out to the TV station and tape that FSU game. The game wasn't on TV, and this was pre-VCR/DVR days, of course.

I had to listen on radio, but I wanted to listen to that game. It was Bobby's debut, and the Seminoles lost the game.

The next week, we went on the air at Channel 27. We wanted to really emphasize local sports. I spent a lot of time with Coach Bowden, doing interviews. I was probably out there every day doing interviews.

Back then, he was young, feisty. He was always great with the media and still is today, even with all the slings and arrows of some of the outrageous sports media.

Bobby would always give us an answer. I had never spent a lot of time around big-time college football, so I didn't know how other coaches reacted. But having worked with two coaches at FSU, the difference between Darrell Mudra and Bobby Bowden was like night and day.

Darrell had a Ph.D. I remember one time with Darrell we had a player who was academically ineligible and on the verge of flunking out of school. Darrell pulled out a 25-page dissertation that he had typed himself on his feelings about eligibility for college athletes and how a college scholarship could bring a student-athlete up to a level he would never achieve had he not had the experience.

He had the report documented, complete with footnotes, but that was Darrell. He coached from the press box; Bobby coached from the sideline. It was two different forms of coaching. In 1978, I was working for Channel 6. FSU didn't go to a bowl game, but that was a great year. We were 8-3, and Bobby was really fit to be tied on that one. He couldn't believe it. What happened was the representative from the Hall of Fame Bowl, the first Hall of Fame Bowl game in Birmingham, Alabama, he was under specific instructions to offer Florida State.

Either his plane was late, or his plane was cancelled. So he rented a car and drove down here at halftime. And the Peach Bowl people were hanging out with FSU's athletic director at the time, John Bridgers.

It was all set. The Peach Bowl people were like, "John, we want you guys in Atlanta." So John ignored the Hall of Fame Bowl representative, who called his boss and asked what he should do, and they decided to offer another team. Well, then the Peach Bowl decided it didn't want Florida State after all, so we were left without a bowl trip. Bobby was fit to be tied.

But as for meeting requests, no one is any better. When I worked with him as producer of the *Bobby Bowden Show*, he never turned down a church that needed him to come over and give testimony.

It used to be frustrating to his secretary, Sue Hall, because he would say, "Tell 'em no. Tell 'em no. I can't make any more trips." And then somebody would give them Bobby's private number, and he'd call Sue and say, "Put me down Sunday, two weeks from now. I'm going to a Baptist church in Pensacola." It used to drive the football office crazy.

I spent six years traveling on the Bowden Golf Tour every spring. I sat at the dais, and some of the greatest memories of my life are going with Bobby on that tour. It was long. We spent six days every week on the road playing golf and doing banquets.

He would get up bright and early on these tour stops and go play golf. Still, to this day, I don't know how he plays so much golf. My hands would get stiff about halfway through this tour. I didn't want to see a golf club. I didn't want to see a golf course. But booster clubs learned they could get big money if they bid for a foursome to play with Coach Bowden.

We would always be the first in line at the buffets at these functions, so we'd get done eating, and there would be some downtime before Bobby spoke. He'd have his napkin out, and he would be drawing Xs and Os on it. It was phenomenal. He was always thinking football. He once said to me, "You never know, Gene, I might come up with a play that might win a football game."

A lot of times, his wife, Ann, would travel with us on the tour. Now, he and Ann are true lovebirds. It's just incredible. I hope when I've been married 50, 60 years that we're the same way, because he treats her like they are still on their honeymoon. It was great to see, a couple who raised six children and had all these grandchildren, and he just treated her like she was the high school prom date. That was neat to see. To me, that's a role model, because you want to treat your wife that way.

Bobby would tell these cornpone jokes at the functions, and everybody would roar. Charlie Barnes is one of the funniest people I know. He'd use his best stuff, and people would just stare at him. No reaction. Bobby would get up there and say, "How y'all doin'?" and everybody would roar. But that's the way it was.

A weekly routine during the season, Gene Deckerhoff tapes a pregame interview with Bobby Bowden. *Courtesy of Ryals Lee, FSU Photo Lab*

A NIGHTMARE DAY BECOMES A BIG BREAKTHROUGH

In 1989, I was down in Tampa for the Florida Dairy Farmers convention. During my stay, I was asked by a radio station if I would be able to do the Tampa Bay Buccaneers' play-by-play, becoming their voice for the following season.

I told the station, "Well, you know I've got a job." I really didn't think they were serious. Turns out it was a legitimate offer. I visited with the management of the station, WRDQ Q-105 FM, and they were serious about me.

I said, "Well, I don't know how I can get from Tallahassee to make it to a game." And they told me, "We can get you to whatever stadium the Bucs play at in time for the games."

I though the contract looked good, and the money they were talking sounded good, but I knew I had to have my boss, Seminole

Boosters Inc., sign off on it. I also had to make sure the athletic director back then, Hootie Ingram, who had set up my position as director of electronic media, would sign off on it.

I also knew I had to get Coach Bowden to sign off on it. The station asked why I needed his permission, and I told them it was because we would be doing some of these shows in the middle of the night.

So I got up with Andy Miller, executive director of Seminole Boosters, and Hootie, and they both listened, understood, and said it was OK to do it.

Then all I needed was to talk to Bobby.

The day I needed to ask Bobby for approval, he traveled to Jacksonville to tape commercials for Ford Motors, one of the main corporate sponsors. The advertising agency assured me that everything would be set up in advance.

The plan was for him to get everything done in a few hours, then return to Tallahassee. I had it set up for him to be on a small plane at seven thirty in the morning, and he was going to be in Jacksonville at eight thirty, then he was going to be home by three o'clock in the afternoon.

OK, so at four o'clock, I called the Bowdens' house. Ann answered the phone. She told me he was not home yet. She said she thought I would have him home by three o'clock.

I said, "Well, sometimes, these guys drag things out."

I didn't tell her this, but what happens is Bobby is always like the guinea pig in these commercials. They bring the Florida, Florida State, and Georgia coaches together.

Ford tied in with all three schools with commercials like: there's a Gator in this Ford; there's a Seminole in this Ford, and so forth. But I had learned earlier that Bobby was the guinea pig, the guy going first and made to wait. Because if the commercial set wasn't ready, Bobby would mill around, be friendly to everybody, talk to everybody, and not be upset.

Now Charley Pell would have turned around, walked out, and never come back. Vince Dooley would have gotten his nose bent out of joint, and the commercial shoot would not have been very good. So they always did Bobby first, and it was always an absolute catastrophe waiting to happen. It happened the same way every year.

But the group had promised me that, this time, they would have everything ready. Of course, they didn't.

So I told Ann, "Well, he's on a private plane; maybe they're just having some travel problems."

I tried to telephone, but I couldn't get the advertising agency on the phone. So I called back to Ann at five o'clock. Bobby was still not home. I called back at six o'clock—still not there. Ann says, "Gene, I'm starting to get worried. Do you think Bobby is all right?"

Remember, back then, nobody had cell phones. All you could do was try to telephone the old way. I tried to reassure Ann that Bobby was OK. I said, "Ann, I'm going to call you back one more time. I'll call back at eight o'clock, and if he's not back by then, we're going to have to put out an alarm."

I call back at 8, and Ann says, "Gene, he's not back yet; it's dark. Gene, I don't what to do." This is really making me mad, and I knew Bobby was really going to be bent out of shape.

As we're talking, Ann says, "Gene, hold on, I hear somebody in the driveway."

Sure enough, it's Bobby.

He gets into their house, picks up the phone, says "Hello" in a tone that let me know he wasn't in a good mood.

I said, "Coach, what happened?"

He said, "Gene, the plane was on time. They picked me up just like you said. But when I got to the video set, the cars weren't even there." Now, keep in mind, this is supposed to be a major production with cars, guys posing as football players, the whole bit.

Bobby says to me, "Well, they had this little tent area where they had some coffee, but, Gene, I thought this was all set up."

So then he says, "What do you need?"

OK, now he's just had this miserable day; he's been up since five o'clock in the morning; and I've got to ask him about doing the Bucs and changing how we do his TV show.

I said, "Well, I've got this chance to do Tampa Bay Bucs football broadcasts."

He's says, "That's the NFL, right?"

"Yes, sir."

"Well, you're still going to do us, right?"

"Yes, sir."

"Well, how come you have to call me?"

"Well, I still have to do your TV show; that's what I'm getting paid to do. And we may have to do this show sometimes at one thirty, two o'clock in the morning or later."

He said, "Gene, I think it's great you'll be doing NFL football. Hey, you just wake me up when we need to start. You might have to wake me up between commercials, but we'll do it. That's fine."

And so we've been doing it that way ever since.

THE GREATEST EXPERIENCE

For my purposes, for my job, Bobby Bowden is absolutely the best you can work with.

Bobby is the best at answering questions and telling you what you want, and he's not evasive. I talk to a lot of football coaches who are so paranoid. They don't want to talk about injuries, players who are hurt, missing, et cetera. Now, Bobby is not going to give away the ranch on information, but he will at least answer the question, and he won't get upset when you ask that type of question. Some coaches get upset with you, thinking the guy doing the coach's show shouldn't be asking such questions.

But Bobby has never gotten upset with any question I've asked. And he's always been ready to tape the show, no matter how late it is.

For example, we played Boston College for the first time in Boston back in September '05. We got back and did the TV show at four thirty in the morning. Bobby slept on the airplane, and he was alert enough to do the TV show, then go home and fall back to sleep.

But that's the way he has always been. Thankfully, unlike me, he doesn't have to drive to Tampa or get back on another airplane to head to a Bucs game.

There are times when the Bucs might have their open date on a Sunday, or they might play a game on a Monday night, and we could do the show at eight o'clock or nine o'clock in the morning that Sunday.

But he's always said, "No, I'd just as soon do it when we get back, I rather do it right away." He wants to go ahead and do it and get it done. And he's a natural at it.

Most college coaches shows you watch now, it's almost as if they protect the coach. They have somebody narrating the plays, they might have a feature on a player, a feature on education, then a comment from the head coach on the next week's opponent, and that's it. The show basically protects the coach, because he's probably not the best in front of a camera or maybe he doesn't want to be in front of the camera.

But Bobby has always done the TV show the way he's done it. He narrates the highlights with a little help from the host. He has an uncanny knack for remembering down and distance.

I always felt this is truly the *Bobby Bowden Show*. Bobby is the show. It's not *Seminoles Football with Bobby Bowden*. And he does a remarkable job. But that's the way Bear Bryant did it. That's the coach's show Bobby watched when he began his career at Samford. He saw Bear Bryant do his show, and Bobby wanted to do it the same way.

Over the years, there have been some funny times on the show. Remember Dedrick Dodge, the cornerback from the late '80s? We were doing the spring game that year, I think, and Bobby was talking about this "Deedrick" Dodge, then he says to watch this guy "Deadrick" Dodge. It goes back and forth like that: Deedrick, Deadrick. And finally I said, "Coach, is it Deedrick or Deadrick?"

Without even stopping, Bobby says, "Gene, it's Dodge."

David Castillo, who played center forever, he told me that he would always watch Coach's TV show, just to hear what Bobby would call him each week. It would be Costello, Castella, Casteo, Costella. It was this ongoing joke with David, and he got a big kick out of it.

But maybe one of the funniest things happened one time when Bobby was feeling a little hoarse. Every year he comes down with a little bit of a cold, maybe in the first month. It goes through his throat and he's hoarse.

I'll come down with the same thing. So that's why I always keep throat lozenges. Bobby saw me put those in my mouth one day.

He said, "Hey, Gene, do those long genes really work?"

I'm thinking, "Long genes?"

"Coach, that's a watch, you know—Longines?"

He's says, "No, long genes for your throat."

Then I realized and said, "Coach, this is a lozenge." And he laughed and told me that he's been calling them "long genes" all his life.

But that's Bobby. I think Bobby is the same coach, the same guy, he has always been.

I know this, I think about it regularly, how fortunate I am to work with the man who may be the winningest major-college coach of all time. I sure say a lot of prayers. It's been a blessing and a pleasure to work with Bobby Bowden.

CHARLIE BARNES

---◄■──────○──────■►---

THE PITCHMAN

Charlie Barnes gets to play Monday-morning quarterback during Florida State's football season. Even the second-guessing is fun. He is the emcee of the weekly Bobby Bowden Booster Luncheon, a role he has deftly handled since 1986. He is the setup man, coaxing a ballroom audience into cheers during a review of the Seminoles' game the past weekend. He'll tell some jokes, pick up snippets from sports sections throughout the state, and then have people excited for a standing ovation when he announces, "Welcome the best football coach in America, Bobby Bowden." If it's a difficult loss, such as to Florida or Miami or to several others the past five years, then Barnes tries to make everyone realize the sun will poke through the clouds again. Life can't stay miserable. There have been two constant elements: Barnes is always funny, and Bowden speaks every week, no matter the outcome. In addition to his day job as executive director of Seminole Boosters Inc., he helps manage the annual spring golf tour with Bowden, where he "Barne-storms" through-out the state and points elsewhere. The role has enabled Barnes to have many private hours with Bowden. No other person, except for Ann Bowden, has had such private access during the past 28 years.

When I accepted a position in 1978 with Seminole Boosters Inc., I was told part of the job was to help organize and expand the Bobby Bowden golf tour. Coach Bowden created the tour when he came to FSU in the spring of 1976; it was his version of the coaches' tour they had at West Virginia. He loves playing golf, so this was a way of getting him around the state, visiting the booster clubs, and helping raise money. Back then, the Seminole Boosters staff consisted entirely of Andy Miller, now president and CEO; a secretary; and later, me.

I was hired to develop new networks outside of Tallahassee, to strengthen the booster clubs, and to work with donors and people throughout the entire state. At that time, the Bowden tour was sort of a hodgepodge affair. It was like feudal Germany: everyone had their own castle and their own rules, and there was no law. The local leaders at each club would orchestrate the show, and there would be singers, dancers, cloggers, and somebody would speak. They worked very hard, and the fans were thrilled to be with fellow Seminoles, but it was endearingly chaotic, and there was no structure to any of it. The banquet might finish before midnight, or it might not.

The one common element, however, was everybody was extraordinarily happy to see Coach Bowden. We had a great many loyal fans who were starved for anything related to Florida State. In fact, a lot of those same people remain involved with Seminole Boosters 30-plus years later.

Over time, we were able to build structure into the entire six-week tour so the relentless travel didn't just completely beat him up. He could have chaos for one day, but if he did it that way every night, night after night, and didn't get to his hotel room until two o'clock in the morning, it would wear him down. It would wear anybody down.

Before I started on the tour that first year, I remember asking my father, "I'm going to be traveling with the head football coach, and I've got to speak. I'm sort of the opening act, and I'll do the introductions. I'm not really sure how to approach this. Do you have any advice for me?"

Dad thought about it for a while and said, "Well, I'll give you two pieces of advice. First, always remember who the star is."

The implication, of course, was that the star was not me.

Then he said, "Second, you have to remember that coaching is a very closed fraternity. When you're watching a football game, always remember that the coaches on the sideline have more in common with the coaches on the other side wearing the different color shirts than they do with the fans in the stands, because they know they're all going to get fired and they are all going to have to hire each other. And they understand each other. They understand what the fans are like."

My father said, "Remember, no matter how long Bobby Bowden is here at Florida State, he will never have the same relationship with fans as he will with other coaches in his profession. That's the nature of their business." And boy, has that proven true.

After I introduced myself, Coach Bowden and I worked out a schedule. I had my car, a garnet Buick Skylark, and that's how we traveled around the state for six weeks every spring.

The first thing he did was put me at ease. He was just a real easygoing guy—very down to earth. I think that's what made us click right away. Also, neither of us like change at all. We both like routine, and we don't like surprises.

I knew my job was to do whatever he wanted to do. Coach Bowden's concept of cooperation and teamwork is everyone doing exactly what he says, all at the same time. Life was simple; we did things exactly the way he wanted them done, and both of us were happy.

We didn't listen to music in the car. We didn't have a radio on. He didn't like that. The trips in the car were usually very quiet, so he would nap. I would drive. We had a clothes rack hooked across the back of my car. Back then, Ann Bowden traveled with us, and poor Ann would have to sit in the back seat and tilt her head under the clothes rack so she could rest.

We used to take cardboard sleeves of Seminole hats to all the golf tournaments. That was the only way our fans could get Seminole merchandise back then. My car trunk would be crammed with sleeves of hats, and the backseat area next to Ann and under her feet would be crammed with stacks of hats. She was such a good sport; that had to be a royal pain for her. Ann never complained.

She wanted to travel with us, and Coach wanted her to be with him. They were real tight. In fact, it seemed like they were still high school sweethearts; they really doted on each other. It was special to see.

I couldn't play golf on the Bowden tour because I had to stay on the telephone to call the next place and the next place and so on. We were on this tour in a long sequence of days and weeks, and remember, this was the pre–cell phone era. I couldn't afford to be isolated and out of touch for four or five hours on a golf course. Sometimes, I would escort Ann out for some shopping or jogging, or we would stop at a 7-Eleven or some kind of convenience store with a pay phone so I could make phone calls.

She was a good sport. She didn't have anything to do during the day and had no transportation. When she was playing tennis regularly, there were times the local booster clubs would host an Ann Bowden tennis tournament in conjunction with the golf event. After the Bowdens started getting grandchildren, she traveled less and less. She had her own schedule.

Nowadays, she'll still occasionally travel with us. Coach Bowden is really happy when she's there. He's always happier when she's nearby.

In the early years of the tour, the evening events lasted much longer. We're always out by 10:00 p.m. now, but back then, the events might go on until 11:00, and it might be midnight before we left town. We'd drive two or three hours to the next town and then spend the night.

Sometimes Coach Bowden would stay awake in the car for hours telling jokes. I always suspected he did it just to make sure I was awake at the wheel. He'd stay up and talk, and then, all of a sudden, I would look over and he would be asleep.

In the car, he and I seldom talked about football. We talked about the other things in which we shared a common interest. We'd talk a great deal about the military and military history. He has a fascination with World War II, and I served in Vietnam. We talked about generals and battles, and of course, that suggests many parallels with coaching and football. We talked about life generally—a whole lot of things.

My success in dealing with him is realizing he is the star and my job is to take care of him. I don't abuse the relationship by asking him the questions that all of us fans would love to know the answers to. I'd like to, but I don't. Maybe I will when we take the final Bobby Bowden golf tour, whenever that time comes.

Now, there was one thing we didn't have in common. He liked to chew tobacco. He especially liked chewing tobacco in my car. He would get a soft-drink bottle, drink most of the soda, and then start

Charlie Barnes (L) and Bobby Bowden before a spring game during the early years of Bowden's tenure at Florida State. Barnes and Bowden are shown here with Andy Miller, president of Seminoles Boosters. *Courtesy of FSU Sports Information*

chewing tobacco and spitting in the bottle. Now remember, that's a small opening. And I had a brand-new car one year. And he was sort of random about hitting the bottle opening.

He was spitting into that bottle and laughing at me, because he thought I was being too fussy about my car. He'd laugh and say, "Uh-oh, I need some more chaw. Go pull into that 7-Eleven so I can get some."

He also would chew on cigars. He never smoked them, but he'd chew on them, and there would be these pieces of cigar tobacco all over the car. We were like the *Odd Couple*. I kept a stump of one of those cigars at home as a memento.

One day as we were riding in the car, he mentioned something about chewing tobacco with his sons. I said, "Hold it. You chew tobacco with your sons? It surprises me you would do that."

He said, "Well, I had four boys. I didn't want them to cuss. And I didn't want them to drink. And I didn't want them to do some other bad stuff. But dadgummit, a boy just has to do something wrong. So I would round them up, and we'd all go sneak out behind the house, away from Ann's sight, and we'd all chew tobacco together. A boy has to do something wrong."

But Dad's there to make sure it all stays within the boundaries.

A PEEK INSIDE THE MIND

I remember the first time I got some insight into his character. We were driving between Tallahassee and Panama City. We passed a high school, and on this day the school was holding its graduation ceremony.

Coach looked out the window and said, "Oh look, they're having graduation over there. That's interesting."

He then paused for a couple seconds and said, "Jeffrey graduated from high school today."

And I thought, "Wow! He has obligated himself to me to go to this booster event, and he's doing that instead of going to his son Jeff's high school graduation." But that's the way he is. If he said he would do it, then he's going to do it. His whole life has taken on that attitude.

Not long after we started traveling together, I was very impressed with the kind of down-to-earth fellow he was, unaffected by the hero-worshiping on the part of our fans. By the time I came back to FSU, Coach Bowden had already beaten Florida once, and we were getting ready to beat them three more times. There was this song about Bowden, produced by this band called Murray and the Gator Giggers. It was a very chip-on-the-shoulder, "everybody always told us we stink, but now we don't, so a pox on you and your kind" sort of song. I liked it.

There was even a cardboard cutout doll made to look like Coach Bowden. And it featured a halo that you could cut out for his head, but it was also big enough that you could drop it down, and it would become a noose, which is why he always brought that up in reference to his sainthood.

But he was hailed everywhere we went. All these people were clapping and dancing because it was all new. We were winning football games again. They all loved Bobby. We were winning football games again after four long years. And they loved his aw-shucks personality and the corny jokes and his air of confidence. It was a near-worshipful thing.

One day, while on some long drive in the Skylark, I asked him about his public persona, about this aura that surrounded him.

I said, "Let me ask you a question: does it bother you that people treat you like that—that they treat you so worshipfully? Doesn't that put too much pressure on you?"

I sort of expected that he might be humble and religious and say something to the effect of "We all have our role to play" or "I'm not really worthy of that"—something along those lines.

But instead he said, "Naw, I like it. I like that. I like to be recognized. I like the praise, and I like these people. But I know the truth too.

"Every coach that is in this business for a long time knows the truth. Tomorrow, it's going to be different. I drop a couple back-to-back games to Florida and Miami, and it's going to be 'How fast can you get out of town?' That's just the way it is. You have to know the reality of the business if you want to survive."

I felt what he was saying was that he appreciated the glory and the trappings of success and he was going to take the good from it. But he was going to keep it all in perspective because he also understood the truth about fans and winning and losing.

LATE-NIGHT POLICE RAID FOR AN AUTOGRAPH

Coach Bowden was treated as a celebrity almost from the beginning, and it was a wondrous thing to watch. The more he won, the more we fans wanted him to be someone he couldn't possibly be.

Those of us who were Seminoles ached for recognition and respect for our school, and we wanted Bobby Bowden to be the next Bear Bryant. Of course, we never wanted to lose to Florida and Miami, either.

Coach took it all in stride and was always gracious even under the most oddball circumstances.

Oddball might be the best word for what happened one night in Wauchula while on the Bowden golf tour. We'd finished our banquet in St. Augustine and had to drive for hours down to Wauchula that night. We finally found our motel, and in those days it might have been the only motel in the county.

The rooms were laid out in the old way: all arranged in a semi-circle facing the road. Across the street was a dark, burned-out building that might have been a Stuckey's or a Howard Johnson's at one time.

It was well after midnight, and the motel office had closed. They'd taped two keys to the front door—one for "Barnes" and one for "Bouten." I smiled and thought, "Well, he's not always the star."

Coach went into his room, and I went into mine. A few minutes later, I heard a loud knocking outside on Coach Bowden's door. I was furious. "Who would be pounding on his door in the middle of the night?" I wondered.

So I angrily opened the door and walked right into two, burly Hardee County Sheriff's deputies. The two fellows were smiling and talking to Coach Bowden.

"Coach Bowden," they said, "It's such a pleasure to meet you."

One of the deputies gestured over his shoulder to the abandoned building across the street.

"We're on a drug stakeout watching this motel, and we saw you drive in. We couldn't believe it was you!"

So here it was, the middle of night, police knocking on his door, and Coach Bowden got up and immediately began carrying on this conversation. It was unbelievable.

The deputies walked back across the street with a couple of auto-graphed photos, happy in knowing that Bobby Bowden was just as nice a man as everybody seemed to think he was.

RIGHT PLACE AT THE RIGHT TIME

One key to Bobby's success that is overlooked is this: everyone forgets that he was 47 years old when he came here. If he had gone to Florida State and played at Florida State, he would have been one of the oldest male alumni of the university. FSU was a distinguished women's university until 1947. Bowden graduated high school in 1948.

But before coming to Tallahassee, Bowden had already been a successful head coach at three other schools. He won at South Georgia

College; he won at Howard College, now Samford; and he won at West Virginia.

He always told me, "I was able to make my mistakes out of sight."

Think about it. Other than local fans and media, nobody paid attention to Howard; nobody paid attention to South Georgia College; and really, West Virginia wasn't prominent on the national media radar.

And he knows there were times as a young coach when he might have made some decisions, might have done some things, that would have severely compromised even a veteran coach in today's spotlight.

Look at three of our all-time top assistant coaches: Brad Scott, somebody I thought could not miss as a head coach; and Gene McDowell, a man I deeply respect. Both struggled as head coaches. And Chuck Amato is going through struggles now. All three of those men went directly from being a top assistant to being the head coach at a Division I program.

As Coach told me once, there is a world of difference between being an assistant coach and being a head coach, and no matter what you think you know, it's very, very difficult to prepare for the responsibility.

He said, "You can study and study, but what I have found is that success is not a very good teacher. But failure is one heck of an instructor."

He fears losing, and that's the key to understanding his particular mentality.

THE PUBLIC SIDE, THE PRIVATE SIDE

As we traveled around the state on the annual tour, the jokes Bobby delivered were always the same. He might even start by saying, "I mighta told this one last year." No one cared. They laughed just as hard at the same jokes year after year.

That was the thing that used to upset Gene Deckerhoff and me. Gene would often travel with us, but in his own van. In between stops, he and I would work on our material and our presentations.

Gene is a very funny and personable guy, and he would be entertaining. I feel like I'm funny and entertaining, too. But we'd get up to the podium, and people would just sit there and politely clap. You could hear a chair scooting, but people were always polite. Nobody got real restless. They were just tolerating us until the headliner got up.

But then we would introduce Bobby, and the audience would break into this roar. It was sort of like, "Oh yeah. Oh man! Bob-by! Bob-by, Bob-by Bow-den!"

And he would stand up there and tell these jokes that I thought were some of the corniest, worst jokes I had ever heard. I thought some were not clever at all, but people would fall off their chairs in hysteria.

Women would faint laughing. Guys fell on the floor. I think Coach Bowden could have read the phone book and they would have laughed. It didn't make any difference.

So Gene and I would look at each other like "Why are we even here?" I mean, we would get up there and get nothing, maybe a polite response. But Gene and I were the commercials before the show.

Coach Bowden has an inspired sense of timing. When he's on and the audience is responding, I've never seen anybody as good as he is. Maybe Robin Williams is as good. Bobby just has that sense of delivery that's natural to him.

Most people don't really understand who he is. For them, it's more of a case of who he wants them to see.

He's not two different guys; he is in fact the man he appears to be. But the only face the fans see is the face he wants to show them. The face he shows the public is a very genuine face, but it's incomplete. His presentation of himself in public is very deliberate.

And there is more to him than they see. He's not a man who lets his guard down. Maybe that's one of those lessons he learned so many years ago in the media backwater.

Coach Bowden can have a hard edge to him that he doesn't let people see. Fans who entertain the idea that Coach Bowden is not tough enough to make the hard decisions don't know what they're talking about. Remember, this is a man who is an intensely private guy. His idea of a good time is to go home to put on a pair of oversize black shorts, lie on the couch, and watch old World War II movies. I think what he learned across his career was that there is a face he needs to show the public, and then he can be himself in private.

He is very sociable, which means he mixes well in company, but he is not social at all. Not at all. There is a difference between the private man and the public man. It's not a great difference to be sure, but it is distinct.

I didn't see that other side right away, because he's a happy-go-lucky guy. He's always upbeat. I'm surprised he doesn't hold a grudge any more than he does. Some people have done him wrong, and he's very cognizant of who has done him wrong, but he doesn't seem to hold a grudge over time. He's willing to eventually let things go.

I do think I understand his psychology. I believe he has trained himself to ignore or eliminate all negative thoughts. I know he's had some tragedy in his life. I know he's had some bitter disappointments like everyone has, but I know that he never wants to dwell on negative things. When we travel together, we don't talk about negative things. He won't dwell on people or circumstances that are bad. When he does listen to music while we're traveling, it has to be up-tempo with a good, strong beat. He's always looking for the sunshine.

I believe that he has convinced himself of the destructive power of negative thought. He confronts problems and doesn't ignore them, but I think he deliberately refuses to allow darkness into his mind.

Other than my father, Bobby Bowden might be the toughest guy I have ever known. And people don't think of him that way. *Tough* is not the first word that comes to mind when people see that grandfatherly face. But let me tell you, he is a tough son-of-a-gun. He is tough physically. He is tough as nails physically and mentally.

I think I have a sense of where that comes from. Most guys in sports are oriented in one of two ways: they are either team oriented like a quarterback, or they are individualists like a boxer.

A quarterback will lose the game and might say something like, "I think we played good as a team, but we lost as a team." It means he can put the loss behind him.

A boxer—and Bowden was a boxer as a young man—knows there is no such thing as a boxing "team." If you get in the ring and you lose, it's because you weren't man enough to get the job done. The boxer has to look within himself for the answers. But when he wins, it's his win and nobody else's win. The boxer knows in his heart that either he won or he lost. And that is Bobby Bowden's mind. He takes his own counsel.

Bowden is the authority of record on a team sport—football—but he is not a team guy in his personal life. He understands he's in a business that is a team business, but his personal psychology is different.

How tough is he? Here's an example.

I remember we were in Pensacola one night for our booster tour. We were sitting at the head table, and he mentioned to me, "I have a bad headache."

Well, that was all I needed; my job was to scurry around for help. I went out in the audience, and I got a couple of Advil. I snuck back to the table, and I had the pills and tried to hand them to him. He just looked at them and asked, "What's that?"

I said, "That's Advil."

He asked, "What does that do?"

I answered, "Well, it will make your headache better."

He shook his head and said, "No, no, I'm not going to take any pills."

You see, in his world, where he came from, I guess pain is weakness. If you're strong enough, you can overcome the pain. And he wouldn't take the Advil. He would rather hurt and be cranky about it, but he was not going to take the pills to help.

"Only if I absolutely can't stand it," he said.

NEVER SHOWING WEAKNESS

Another spring, soon after we had won that second national championship, I took Coach Bowden to play Old Memorial Golf Club in Tampa. It was a private club, a really elite golf course that had just opened. This was not a booster function; it was a private round with some major donors.

I dropped off Coach Bowden with our former All-American receiver Barry Smith, who is a loyal supporter and close friend of Coach Bowden. He is one of the most generous donors to our athletic program.

I then drove into downtown Tampa on probably the hottest day of the year. It was unbelievably hot. What I didn't know was that Old Memorial Golf Club was not allowing use of golf carts. Either they didn't have the carts because the club was new, or it was the club policy.

In any case, it meant that everyone, Coach Bowden included, had to walk the 18-hole round in that relentless heat.

Uh-oh.

When I got back to the clubhouse, I headed for the shade of the veranda, sipped a cool drink, and waited for the group to finish the 18th hole. I was waiting to hear the rumble of golf carts, which didn't exist.

And that's when I saw Barry Smith coming across the sandy brush. His face was bright red. His hair was going in three different directions. He was dragging his clubs behind him.

Understand, Smith is a stud athlete, a first-round draft pick still in fighting shape in his mid-fifties. Coach Bobby Bowden was in his seventies and nowhere in sight.

Barry came up the steps, and he was out of breath, exhausted, and I said, "Barry, what in the world happened?"

He said, "I'm really sorry. I didn't realize they wouldn't let us use a cart."

I said, "Holy smokes! Where's Bobby?"

Well, about that time, Coach Bowden came into view, walking off the 18th hole, and he had this real grim face. He walked straight across the road to the clubhouse veranda and stared at me.

Barry said, "Coach, would you like to go into the clubhouse and have something cool to drink?"

Bowden looked straight at me, not smiling, and said, "Charlie, you got the van ready? Let's get in the van."

Barry glanced at me and whispered under his breath, "Apparently not."

I tried to keep from smiling.

So I put him in the van, and we left the course, and after a while I pulled over to a convenience store and bought him a cold drink. He had to have been dying from four hours in that heat, but he wouldn't admit it. He wouldn't complain. He wouldn't say a word. But I knew that it would be very wise of me to ensure this type of situation never happened again.

But again, here was Coach Bowden, already in his seventies, who had just walked 18 holes in all that heat, then had to get ready to give a speech that night. Oh yeah, he also had to play another round of golf the next day.

But that's really Bobby Bowden in a snapshot. He has exceptional strength of mind along with the unique physiology that enables him to be tough. He can play golf, no matter the conditions, finish the round, then quickly recover for a banquet speech. As long as he can get back to a hotel room for a shower and take his nap for an hour or two, he can regenerate his physical strength.

When you stop and think about it, the more amazing he becomes. But Bobby Bowden is the toughest nice guy I have ever known.

WARRICK DUNN

⊷•⊷═⊷•○•⊷═•⊷

THE ADOPTED SON

Of the story lines connected with Florida State's 1993 national title season, none may be more poignant than that of Warrick Dunn. His impact as a freshman tailback went beyond rushing yards or big plays. He touched lives. Once FSU fans learned of his personal tragedy, the loss of his mother, Betty, a Baton Rouge police officer killed in a robbery in January 1993, Dunn became a sentimental favorite. His mother's death came two days after his 18th birthday. He signed with FSU a month later, moved in with quarterback Charlie Ward, and the two became a dynamic playmaking duo. Arguably the greatest play of Dunn's career came on November 27, 1993, against Florida in Gainesville. Facing third-and-10 from the FSU 21 late in the fourth quarter, Dunn caught a swing pass from Ward, broke a sideline tackle, picked up a block, and outraced the Gators defenders into the end zone for a game-sealing touchdown. The win enabled FSU to play for its first national title in the Orange Bowl against Nebraska. Dunn finished as the Seminoles' all-time leading rusher (3,959) and was their last 1,000-yard rusher. He begins his 10th NFL season in 2006 as the top running back for the Atlanta Falcons. Along with his football achievements, Dunn is equally renowned for his philanthropic efforts, helping build homes for single mothers, along with various other charities through the Warrick Dunn Foundation.

What's funny about my first contact with Coach Bowden and Florida State is that I really did not follow the Seminoles in high school. Of course, everybody at school, all my friends, would watch

the Miami–Florida State games and stuff like that, but I just didn't
grow up watching Florida State at all. I think for me, once I started
getting recruited by FSU, then I began paying attention a little bit.

My recruiting trip was the first time I met Coach Bowden. The
way it works, you hook up with a current player, and I was with receiver Kez McCorvey a lot. I think I first met him on the one day
when all the players meet the coach, which is usually on a Saturday
during recruiting visits. That's when teams say how much they want
you there.

When I first saw Coach Bowden, it reinforced his mystique
because he walks slowly—just because of the way he looks. My mouth
was kind of wide-open. There I was, visiting Florida State, and then I
got to see the legend at the same time.

I think at that particular time in my life, because I had just lost my
mom, I didn't know what to expect. I didn't really care. I was in awe a
little bit, but at the same time, I wasn't really wowed by anything. I was
still trying to deal with my personal life.

Of course, I wanted to connect with a coach who could understand my situation—somebody who hopefully could teach me at the
same time. The visits I made to other schools were good, and I was
comfortable with some of the coaches. But when I went to Tallahassee,
I just felt like it was right. It was a case of, "OK, I lost my mom; this
feels like home." It was just like home.

One of the things I immediately liked about Coach Bowden was
just listening to his accent. His accent is the funniest thing. And once
you're there and he really can't remember all the players' names, that
makes it more hilarious. I know he called me Warren the whole time.
So it was stuff like that. It's those kind of things about him that you
pick up on, because deep down, in his background, he is a true, good
ol' country, Southern guy.

Every team was recruiting me as an athlete or a defensive back. I
just tried to convey to Coach Bowden that if I decided to come to
FSU, I wanted to play tailback first. He understood that.

Once I signed, the coaches said, "Well, you can start off at running
back, and if doesn't work out, you can move to defensive back." That
was fine for me. I felt like as long as I had the opportunity to go out

and see if I could do it, to show them I could be a running back, that's all I needed.

So I guess after the second or third practice my freshman year, they realized I wouldn't be going to any other position. I never lined up one play at cornerback. And to be honest, I didn't play cornerback that much in high school. I started at cornerback when I was a junior in high school, but I started at quarterback when I was a senior. Really the only time I played cornerback was in certain situations in our territory. I just wasn't really keen on hitting people.

Looking back now, one of the things that strikes me is that Coach Bowden is a man of his word. The thing is, you might not really think Coach Bowden remembers everything because he's old and he has got a lot going on, but he does remember everything. I think that's an amazing thing.

Before I signed with Florida State, and I think it was after I took my recruiting visit, he actually came to Baton Rouge, came to the house, sat down in the living room, and said all those things to me. He lived up to everything he said he would do.

A SECOND FATHER

When I look back on my time at Florida State and getting to know Coach Bobby Bowden, I have to say he wasn't just a coach; he was also a father figure. He was somebody I could lean on whenever I needed support because I needed him to be that way. He was that kind of person to me.

He tried to say, "If you need me, I'm there." It wasn't any pressure or anything he tried to force. He tried to just let me come into my own, but if I made mistakes on the football field, he would let me know that too.

Away from the field, he always let me know his office door was open and that I needed to utilize it. He told me, "I've had a lot of sons, and I've been through a lot of things, and I have a lot of advice that can be useful for you."

I went to him throughout my years at Florida State. He didn't make the decisions for me, but he gave me a lot of examples and put me in a lot of situations that helped me make good, sound decisions.

If I needed to leave, to go back home to Baton Rouge, I could always leave. Coach Bowden understood that, and he knew that for me, my brothers and sisters were much more important than anything else that was going on in my life.

I think that says a lot about him. To me, that shows it's not just about the game of football we play, but it's about life. You think about all the wins, all the great players, all the great teams; but to him, family is first, then football. I can respect that. And today I still live by that. My feeling is that if something happens with someone in my family, forget football; it's just a game. I can always come back.

When I was at Florida State with Coach Bowden, I just think it was an understanding. We didn't have set rules and guidelines, but it was an understanding while I was there. If something happened and I went to talk to him, he understood and he tried to help me the best way he could. He couldn't give me money or put me on a private jet, but he would always say, "If you need to do something, you have to take care of your brothers and sisters."

I would talk to him about anything, about my sisters, dating—anything. I would talk to him about my other brothers and sisters and how they were doing in school. I talked to him about everything going on in my life. Remember, I was trying to deal with my mother's death and all the memories. Coach Bowden was just somebody who was real compassionate. He took time away from his own busy schedule to be there for me.

We all know how busy he is, but I could call him at home, at work; he would always get back to me. So it was something I will always cherish. I became like a son to him.

I can say for me, at that particular time in my life, he helped me tremendously. For me, he was probably that missing piece that I needed to just stay sane. He was one of the few guys I could sit and talk to. I had Charlie Ward, who I could call at any time, but talking with Coach Bowden was different. He had kids, and they were all successful, so he had a lot of stories and wisdom and knowledge to share. It was great to have him in my life.

Warrick Dunn, sharing a laugh with Bobby Bowden before the Seminoles 2006 spring game, is grateful for the values he learned under his former coach. *Courtesy of Glenn T. Beil*

He did help me with my sisters, to know how to be friends with them and understand what they were going through—not necessarily to be strict, but to be understanding. All my sisters now, we're best friends. My oldest sister, she moved with me when I played for the Bucs. I had given her a lot of responsibility.

It's crazy. I don't know what my life would have been like if I hadn't had a guy like Coach Bowden—if I hadn't had him there for me.

The thing with Coach Bowden is he never told me, "This is what you really need to do." He tried to put things to me in basic English. He would say, in effect, "These are the things I had to go through with my kids." And I just took that and built my own conclusions on what to do with my own family.

Sometimes, the best teacher is someone who gives you a bunch of examples and allows you to figure things out on your own. I tried to do that all the time. Even with my brothers and sisters. I gave them choices. My youngest sister is now 22, so just imagine what I was dealing with back then.

But anytime I needed Coach Bowden, I don't care if it was off-season or during the season, anytime I needed him, he was there.

Now I call him and ask what's going on, what's up with the program. We talk about players, and I ask him to tell this guy to do this or that—not just me, but all the former players. We're always concerned about the program and the direction it's going. I feel like I was one of the guys who helped build the legacy. Coach Bowden is happy guys are concerned about it, and he wants the younger guys to know that it's a tradition we helped build and these guys on the team now have to carry it on.

I remember when we played Virginia in 1995 on that Thursday night game. I had to be in court the next day in Baton Rouge, so I had to leave right after the game. I had to miss class and everything else, and he let me leave. That's one thing I will always remember.

I wanted to be in court because it was during the sentencing phase of the trial for the guys who shot my mother. I wasn't there at any time during the trial, but I felt like it was important that I came and testified. The people all knew I had had a game the night before. Of course, in that game against Virginia, I got into the end zone. I scored. I just want that on the record.

When I got back in town, Coach Bowden sat all of us down, the juniors and seniors, and said, "We lost to Virginia, and we shouldn't have lost this game." We just didn't play well, and you could tell he was concerned a little bit. He said we needed to turn things around. Before that game, we all felt like we had a chance to play for a national championship. We had been playing well.

A COACH'S INTUITION

Everybody, I think, knows the story of how the coaches got me to room with Charlie Ward my freshman year. Rooming with Charlie Ward was like a match made in heaven; he was a guy who had been through so much on his own to be the starting quarterback at Florida State.

Charlie's whole demeanor was the right fit for me. We were so similar, and I just had so much emotion and feeling built up inside of me. He was definitely the person I needed at that particular time. The first time I talked to Charlie on the phone, we talked for 30 or 40 minutes. Now, you don't talk to a complete stranger for that long, but we hit it off over the phone. And when I met him in person, I tried to mimic him a little bit.

I think the coaches felt a guy like me, who had just lost his mom and was dealing with a lot, needed to be with somebody who could help. They felt like Charlie would be that guy. They felt like I had the same characteristics as Charlie, and they were right.

That's just an example of how Coach Bowden notices things and has a certain feel for a situation. As a player, you see him up in the tower on the practice field. But you don't realize when he's in the coaches' meetings, he's coaching the coaches. You realize when you ask him about this play here or that play there, that he truly understands the game of football and completely knows what we're doing week in and week out. I think that's a lot for any coach.

Not only does he have to know the players, but offensively, Coach Bowden is very involved. He studies film all the time. I have walked into his office many times when he has turned away from the desk and cut the film off, because he was watching film. I would think to myself, "Well, he's doing what assistant coaches do, but he's the head coach, watching all this film." I just have so much respect for him.

When I get married, I will call Coach Bowden, and, hopefully, he will be able to come to my wedding. I feel like he's that important to me. A big event like that in my life. I will ask him to my wedding.

I invited him to my NFL Man of the Year award because he was one of the most important figures in my life that helped me get to that point.

When I look back at all I've been through in my career—being undersized and having to answer those questions about my ability—I had to prove to him I could do it. Before my sophomore year, I spoke to him about getting more carries. As a freshman I had about 500 or so yards. I think we happened to be walking back to the Moore Center, or maybe it was right before our first game, when I asked Coach Bowden, "When is the last time you had a 1,000-yard rusher? I think I can get it."

He was like, "OK." At the time, I don't think he really believed me. I just knew from that point on, I was going to go out and get 1,000 yards. That was my determination. I felt that if I rushed for 1,000 yards at Florida State, I would really have done something special as a running back. So that was my goal. That's what I set out to do. That year, I rushed for more than 1,000 yards.

There are not too many coaches I have played for who I didn't want to let down. There haven't been too many coaches who I always wanted to play hard for. But Coach Bowden was one of them. The other might have been my little league coach in Baton Rouge.

I just felt like Coach Bowden gave so much to me, personally, that I was going to go out and leave it all on the field for him. When we lost a game, I didn't just feel bad for myself and my teammates. I felt bad for him because I knew that he had to answer all the questions about why we lost.

I think everybody on our team, over time, developed that kind of respect for Coach Bowden. It was a case of, if we lost a game, we cared how he felt, how he was going to be treated.

That's another thing I love about him. All the accolades and everything else—you don't think about a guy who is talking about himself in terms of "I'm all this," "I'm coach of the year," or "I did this or that." And I think, over the years, it has rubbed off on different players or different teams that we don't have to boast about how great we are and we don't have to boast about all the things we do. Because if we play well, others will make a fuss about it for us.

The week we played Florida for the national championship game in the Sugar Bowl, we got out of character a little bit. I felt like our defense got on television too much, talking about, "We'll just keep hitting Danny Wuerffel." That had been the big deal before the game.

Our guys didn't normally do that, and I felt like we got out of character. I mean, we were a great team, and we should have just played and let that take care of it. We talked a lot before we played. I think Coach Bowden may have learned from that experience too. It should have been a case of, "Guys, let your football speak for itself."

OVERCOMING ADVERSE TIMES

The 1993 season, when we won our first national championship, was special. There was so much that happened.

We were kind of rolling along until that Notre Dame game. That was the game where Coach Bowden chastised me in front of the whole team. We were playing at Notre Dame, in South Bend, and guys were slipping down. Everybody was falling.

At halftime, he called me out in front of the whole team. I was stunned. I was thinking, "What the heck? Charlie's out there slipping; Derrick Brooks is out there slipping. Call those guys out."

But Coach Bowden said, "Warrick, you ain't no freshman anymore. You're not in high school anymore. You have to play big-time." He got on me, and he challenged me at the same time. I will always remember that. He knew the potential I had.

He didn't usually call guys out. He wasn't like that. He didn't point the finger. He always tried to be encouraging. But at that time, that game, I guess it was the No. 1 versus the No. 2 team in the country. And it seemed like everybody on our team was falling down. I think he thought this was the best way to get everybody's attention. He was saying, "I have to pick on the youngest guy and say he has to step out."

About that field—people have said they thought Notre Dame let the grass grow or soaked the field. All I know is we went out there the day before the game, and that field was nice, and it was dry. The next day, it was slippery and wet. Now, it didn't rain, and I know there's not that much dew on the ground, so you do wonder.

We lost the game, but the next week Notre Dame lost and we killed NC State, so we were back in it. Then we played Florida. We were winning, but Florida got back in the game, and we had to make a play. It was a third-down pass from Charlie.

The thing was, it was just a basic swing pass in the flat. I don't know how many times we ran that play, but it couldn't have been more than four or five. On that particular play, I was open, caught the ball, and was able to break a tackle and score. I was so worried they were going to call a clip on Tamarick Vanover, but they didn't.

I have pictures of that play in a sequence in a frame at my house in Baton Rouge. Everywhere I go, people ask me about that play. They always remember that play. I guess that's how I will be remembered at Florida State, and it's a good way to be remembered.

The night we won the national championship, beating Nebraska in the Orange Bowl, it was just crazy in our locker room—really crazy. But you could just see what it meant by looking at Coach Bowden's face. After all those years of being close, all those wide rights, wide lefts, it was like a feeling of relief on his face. It was like a feeling of, "I can breathe again." He handles everything gracefully. I just think the way he handled that, it was so respectful. It was top-notch.

We were all running crazy, but you can just see he wanted to share that moment with his wife and the players. Obviously, he knew that we had been through so much that whole season. He wanted to share it with the players and his wife, Ann. I remember he gave her this deep kiss, and all the players in the locker room were going crazy. He was just like that. He loves her so much. He put her in our playbook, believe it or not. She had her own plays in our playbook. We had a running play called Ann.

NECESSARY LESSONS FOR THE NFL

I didn't think I'd play in the NFL until after my junior season. That's when people thought I would leave and go pro. I always thought I was too small. I also felt like in the NFL, somebody would want to make me a return specialist or something like that, and I just wasn't really feeling that.

At the time, my whole thing was family. I was still in the family mode, not really worrying about the NFL.

Florida State prepares you for the NFL indirectly. The type of system Coach Bowden has at Florida State, the workout regimen he demands, the way we practice, it's all good training for the NFL.

It's a team concept—play as a team—but great players have always been recognized, so Coach Bowden was able to convey how we needed to just play within the team. He really tried to train our minds. You would think about being successful, making a great catch, a great tackle, a great run. Coach Bowden always talked about greatness. He always talked about being great.

At Florida State, if you don't play hard, there's a guy right behind you who can take your position. The night before a game, Coach Bowden always gave you something to think about, something that really helped you out. When you went back to your room, you would start dreaming about it—at least I did.

Faithwise, Coach Bowden left quite an impression. When you see the head coach really step out in his faith and in everything he does, it really opens your eyes to a lot of things. Usually, a head coach is the opposite of what the players are. Coach Bowden was the same guy. For me, that's where I got closer to the Lord. It was during my freshman year.

When you see the head coach, and he's attending church, reading the Bible, and having Bible study, it's easy to convince a young kid that that is the right thing to do.

Coach Bowden's a good ol' country boy, Southern swagger, but down to earth, someone who is real, a Christian man. He is just somebody who everybody can relate to. He's a person I respect day in and day out. I could go on and on, trying to describe what kind of person he is.

Whenever I have kids, I think I will take on a lot of things I've been through, take on all the memories I have and all of the advice in the stories he gave me. He's been the one coach, the person in my life who has given me a million stories. If I didn't have a father, Coach Bowden would be like a perfect dad, because he would be understanding yet strict at the same time. I will take all the things I have learned, and hopefully, I will be a good father. He also taught me how to be a better husband, just because of the way he and his wife were.

He was strict. He was stern in his decisions. But he was fair. Since he had teenage boys, he could really relate to a lot of things we were going through as teenagers. When guys were in college, the feeling was, "Stay out of trouble, don't let it get back to Coach Bowden, and you'll be OK."

If somebody had never met him before and asked me what he was like, I would say, "He is one of the greatest people that I know." That's the best way I know to describe him.

Celebrate the Heroes of Florida Sports
in These Other NEW and Recent Releases from Sports Publishing!

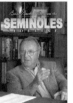